SHUT THE BUT UP!®

~~Boss Babe~~
J. Minor

Copyright © 2021 BossBabe T. Minor

Author Tammy Minor
Cover Design Tonya Jones
Copy Editor Casandra Broaddus
Author Photograph Ariel Moriah

All rights reserved. No portion of this book may be reproduced, stored in a retrieval system, or transmitted in any form or by any means – electronic, mechanical, photocopy, recording, scanning, or other – except for brief quotations in critical reviews or articles, without the prior written permission of the author.

ISBN 978-1-7374772-1-1

Published in the United States

Dedicated To:

First, I'd like to thank **me**. I thank me for believing in me...lol, just kidding (or not). @SnoopDogg

To my children, **Malachi & Arianna**, for being my driving force, the reason I had no other choice than to be a badass boss babe. After all, it was my job to set the right example!

To my husband **Maurice**, (Dominique if he introduces himself or Billy if we are in a foreign country, partying like rock stars) for being so loving, supportive, and of course for the daily Starbucks!

To **Tonya**, the Robin to my Batman. Much appreciation for pushing me to finally write the dang book. Thanks for all the other things you do all day every day to keep me in line and my businesses running!

To **Mila**, our 8lb fur baby, for being the shadow I always wanted.

Last ~~but~~ certainly not least...

...an overwhelming amount of gratitude for **ALL** the bullies, naysayers, toxic family members, and conditional friendships; without you and the fire you put inside me, none of this would be possible!

Hey, BOSS!

I am so <u>excited</u> & <u>honored</u> that you picked up this book ;)

Let me be completely transparent on how I got here: I didn't come from much and always wanted more. I've made mistakes that have set me back a time or two, ~~but~~ no matter what, I still wanted more for myself and my family. I wanted more experiences and adventures than I had growing up. I wanted to be able to give my kids the things they needed (and wanted) that I never had. And although money doesn't buy happiness, it sure does fund the ability to do all the things! J/s!

I recognized early on that most people's excuses were greater than their dreams. ~~But~~ no one is perfect, right? And there have been times when I too believed it was easier to fall into the "~~BUT~~" trap than it was to *shut the but up!®*, to do what needed to be done to do better, to accomplish more, and to keep leveling up!

After years of achieving great success, accomplishing goals, and fulfilling my dreams, I frequently get approached by people asking me HOW do I do it. It seemed, more often then not, the very people seeking inspiration, who say they want to make changes, generally all responded with "~~BUT~~...," as if there are reasons success isn't possible for them.

That's why I am here, to help you realize that YOU are the only thing standing in your way. The only thing that you are a victim of... is yourself. The only thing keeping you from accomplishing your goals and dreams is your refusal to *shut the but up!®*

I have laid out these stairs for you because success isn't just "5 Rules" or "25 Secrets", or whatever other book you've read. It's not just about focusing on one area, its working on the WHOLE YOU from the inside out and even around you.

So, are you ready to *shut the but up!®*, to #LevelUp? Let's make it happen!

xoxo – T. Minor

"THERE IS NO ELEVATOR TO SUCCESS.
YOU HAVE TO TAKE THE STAIRS."
-ZIG ZIGLAR

#1 SHUT THE BUT UP!®

WHEN PRESENTED WITH A SOLUTION, HOW OFTEN DO YOU RESPOND WITH ~~"BUT"~~?

It is so easy to do! You know, say "~~but~~" to the things that make us uncomfortable, the things that we are afraid to do. Have you considered, though, that those very things could be the differentiator between the life you are living right now, and the one that is living in your head?

I want you to think of one thing that you want to accomplish. One of those sooner-than-later kinda things. I want to lose a few pounds, for example. So, if I were to consult a trainer or nutritionist, they might suggest I get more sleep, exercise regularly, and cut out Starbucks. Instead of making the changes they've advised necessary to lose weight, it would be easier perhaps to respond with "~~BUT~~, I can't live without my Starbucks." Focusing more on the thought of a day without my favorite magic bean water...shutting down, and throwing the whole idea away. Easier, initially anyway. But what changes? Is it easier long term if my refusal to change keeps me from my goal and begins to affect my health?

The words that follow the "~~but~~" are the excuses, everything about growth that makes us uncomfortable. The words that come behind "~~but~~" go against our habits and routines. It is hard to let go of the safety blankets. We already know how they make us feel. They are also what is holding us back from our greatness. They determine whether you achieve your goals or stay where you are.

We have to *shut the but up!®* in order to level up. We are about to continue up a steep flight of stairs, and we can't take that word with us!

#2 DRINK THE WATER.

HOW OFTEN ARE YOU HYDRATING?

Water is the answer to most of our problems. We all know this, and yet a shocking amount of the population struggles to consume enough.

Research tells us it's a battle for more than half of adults in the United States, and I have been one of them! Turns out, that previously mentioned magic bean water (the stuff that gives me the power to do all the things) doesn't count – rude!

The reasons (excuses) documented are: too busy, we forget, or we simply aren't sure because we don't keep track. When I randomly surveyed people about their *consistent* water consumption (or lack thereof), I found that most felt like they got overwhelmed with the quantity of water they've been told to consume.

This will make you feel better about the task – you do NOT need to drink a gallon of water a day! You do, however, need to drink water every day. You need to study your consumption and find the amount that is right for you. Overhydration is a thing and surprisingly many people aren't even aware of it. The symptoms are much like those of dehydration. They can both affect your energy, brain functions, physical performance plus so much more.

I am sure you've heard before that water is a cure-all.

Thirsty? Drink water.
Tired? Drink water.
Want to lose weight? Drink water.
Want clear skin? Drink water.
Want to get rid of someone? ... J/k!

The list goes on and on. If you want to level up and live your best life, you have to *shut the but up!®* and drink the water! Do you want to make it up these stairs? You are going to have to stay hydrated!

#3 TRUST THE PROCESS.

ARE YOU STILL LOOKING FOR A SHORTCUT?

That's because there are no shortcuts. TBH, even if there were - they aren't worth it! What you discover on the journey is the best part. Could you imagine a movie or a book having like two sentences?

Let's pretend we are going to see a movie about a 10-year-old girl that was born into a poor family in the country and decides she wants to grow up to be famous and live in a big city. Here is what that script would look like:

1. **GIRL IS 10 – DAY**

Girl is 10, sitting outside on a tree stump, swatting away mosquitos, staring into a forest of trees.

> GIRL
> I want to be famous and live in a big city when I grow up.

2. **GIRL IS ADULT – DAY**

Girl is grown up, famous, and living in a big city. She is in her penthouse, staring out of the window at the skyline.

> GIRL
> I did it!

3. **END SCENE**

0/5 stars. Do not recommend. Worst movie ever! We all want to know; what is she famous for? How did she do it? What did she have to overcome to achieve her goals? We don't even know what city she is living in... Leveling up is about trusting the process and enjoying the journey. The journey is where your growth happens. There are no shortcuts! Just *shut the but up!®* and keep climbing!

#4 LET IT GO!

WHY ARE YOU STILL HOLDING ON TO THE PAIN?

Why do you refuse to let it go? Whatever "it" is, what about it has you still holding on so tightly? Maybe it's hard for us to let go because we don't want to lose those parts of our past, we don't want to lose those pieces of ourselves.

IMO, that is emotional hoarding! I know –trust me– I know it is hard! It is painful. It is frustrating. Instead of accepting what happened, we look for ways to make sense of it. We look for ways that we could've changed the outcome. We are confused at the fact that what we give to others simply isn't returned to us.

This might just be one of the hardest stairs to climb, and the obstacles it presents will look different for everyone. What you are holding onto could be so many things. Let me take a few guesses: toxic family member(s), a close friend who did you wrong, an abusive spouse, etc. I understand.

What you are holding onto actually, is your own expectations. The way you think it should've worked out. Unfortunately, it is (most likely) in the past and there is nothing you can do about it. The holding on is in your mind, and you are the only one that has the power to let it go.

As you climb higher up these stairs, the burden of what you are holding on to is going to get heavier and heavier. If you don't *shut the but up!®* and let it go, it will slow you down. Don't let it hold you back.

#5 FORGIVENESS, ALWAYS.

DO YOU REALIZE THAT FORGIVENESS IS FOR YOUR OWN BENEFIT?

It's true. Forgiveness doesn't provide benefits for the receiver of said forgiveness. What it will do though, is keep you from stumbling back down a few stairs. If you've already let it go before you got to this point – Good. For. You! That means that you have forgiven (woohoo)! If reading these words made you sigh, then we have some work to do here so that you don't fall back.

Maybe you are wondering, *how do I know if I have truly forgiven?* A few signs would be a clearer mental state, less anxiety, reduced stress, and a sense of peace.

If you realize that you haven't actually forgiven them yet, let me help you out. First, make sure you let yourself feel all the things and be patient with yourself as you learn the process.

Get mad. Grieve. Get it out – writing a burn letter is really good for this! Set boundaries. SN: Forgiveness doesn't mean that you must continue to have that person in your life.

Now, be your own hero! The only person that is guaranteed to ever save you is YOU. Forgiveness is rescuing yourself. Give yourself a pat on the back for the work you are putting in, take a quick stretch, and let's keep climbing!

#6 NO REGRETS.

HAVE YOU FOUND THE SILVER LINING?

Random – anyone else instantly think of that "NO RAGRETS" tattoo? The meme that went viral a while back. No? Just me? Ok.

Regrets are pointless. Look, if you are the one that made the mistake, bad choice, etc. – you can't change it. Make sure you've apologized and now that you know better, do better. If you are the one who was wronged – you can't change that either. All you have is the lesson learned and the new boundaries you've set. As long as you don't fold on them (the boundaries), then keep climbing upward.

The silver lining is what I like to look forward to. The easiest way for me to talk myself into doing the work to get through the "letting it go" and "forgiveness, always" is telling myself that my track record of surviving the pain is 100%. Reminding myself that the after has always been greater than the before.

There is a great amount of weight lifted off you at this point, can you feel it? Are the stairs getting easier to climb? Are you catching your breath a bit? When it gets tough remember to *shut the but up!®* and keep going!

#7 BE GRATEFUL.

HAVE YOU EXPRESSED GRATITUDE FOR YOUR JOURNEY?

I am about to get vulnerable with you. This story might help you up this stair feeling less alone, might help you climb with more certainty and gratitude than you thought possible.

Throwing it back to 2012, what I once believed would be the worst year of my life. I was married. Who once was Prince Charming, had at this point turned into my worst nightmare. A year or so prior to this is when the mental abuse started, then it became verbal, by this time it was physical. Trying to figure out how to leave him with my life intact and my children safe was proving to be a challenge since he controlled everything. Then, on a

Wednesday afternoon, as I was driving and plotting my next move, life added a challenge on top of a challenge: I get t-boned. A car smashed into my driver's side door, leaving me with some pretty bad spinal injuries. This would lead to a risky surgery, a year and a half of physical therapy 3-4 times a week, and tons of out-of-pocket costs. Geez, that certainly didn't make figuring out how to leave any easier. If you asked me then, I wasn't exactly grateful for any of these things happening to me. At that time, let me tell it, my life was ruined.

Ask me now! I am grateful for all of it! I got away from the crazy man with my life and my kids safe. I got into the supplemental insurance business to protect people from the financial devastation that I experienced when unexpected events happen. I am happily remarried to my best friend. Bonus, I get to share my story with you!

Believe it or not, all the things – the good, the bad, the ugly – all built the unstoppable person you are today. Could you imagine how boring the climb would be without all the unexpected twists and turns? Take a moment to be grateful for even the ugly parts.

#8 SMILE.

YOU DO KNOW THAT IT IS HARDER NOT TO, RIGHT?

Ok ok, when researching, I couldn't find a definitive answer to the old saying that it takes fewer muscles to smile than to frown. The number of muscles used for each, in every article, was inconsistent and all over the place. Lame.

However, smiling immediately improves your mood and decreases stress. That is a scientific fact! It also takes less effort, and, more importantly, less of a toll on your physical and mental health.

Don't say that there is nothing to smile about. First of all, YOU are your own reason to smile. For that alone, you should be smiling more and smiling often. The fact that you are even reading this book tells me that you love yourself and you believe in yourself – so smile for that, dang it!

Second, find more reasons to smile. Find joy in the little things that make you happy. Like those super cute tiny bottles of hot sauce, or that first sip of your favorite Starbucks. What about those first few minutes after you clean and everything is perfect because no one has touched anything yet? How about when you get to sneak in a new house plant without your partner noticing? Can't be just me...

The point is – smile. Smile more. Smile often. Smile for yourself. Smile for no reason. Right now. Smile. Because you've learned to *shut the but up!®* and climbed this far, and you're getting stronger. So, smile.

#9 BE KIND.

WHAT WAS YOUR LAST RANDOM ACT OF KINDNESS?

No, this section isn't solely about being kind to strangers. I just want you to start thinking about it. The awareness alone will most likely result in you unconsciously being more kind to yourself and others.

Much like smiling, kindness is also scientifically proven to improve your overall health. It eases anxiety, releases those feel-good hormones, and reduces stress. This will naturally improve your heart health and prevent illness. I think we just added more years to your life!

There are some easy ways you can be kinder to yourself on a daily basis:

Give yourself "ME" time.
Take care of yourself.
Respect yourself.
Forgive yourself.
Trust yourself.
Love yourself.

You are only guaranteed to ever have yourself to depend on, so be kind to yourself!

Regarding kindness to strangers – you never know the battles they are fighting and how one simple act of kindness could change their life. In the worst of times, a little compassion could be the difference between life or death for someone. Be kind.

You will need kindness to yourself and possibly even from a stranger to help you keep climbing.

#10 FAITH.

WHEN WAS THE LAST TIME YOU TOOK A LEAP OF UTTER FAITH?

"For we walk by faith, not by sight."
–2 Corinthians 5:7

Anyone ever notice how literal this scripture is if you really think about it? This is my life motto. Regardless of your religious beliefs, this is powerful stuff!

Faith = complete trust. It is never wavering. Having complete faith means you don't lose it. You don't wake up and decide to give it up.

I told you that I survived 2012. Faith got me out of there. Faith made it possible for me to decide to leave my J.O.B. in July of 2014 as a single parent on a search for something fulfilling. Faith had me turn down 25+ J.O.B. offers. Faith had me getting my health insurance license and going into a field that I had NO knowledge or experience in, other than what it looked like when I didn't have my own supplemental benefits. Faith had me doing this on a 100% commission basis. Faith has multiplied my revenue year over year. Faith has put me in the category of the "less than 6% of women business owners that make over 6 figures." Faith has grown my brokerage and kept me in business for the last seven years.

I say it was all faith because it wasn't easy, it wasn't always pretty, and there were plenty of days that would have made most people walk away. Faith will separate you from the regular people. Faith will take you to the next level. Faith will make you flourish in your passion and purpose. Faith will silence the excuses, helping you to *shut the but up!®* and get you up these stairs.

#11 COUNT YOUR BLESSINGS, NOT YOUR TRIALS.

ARE YOU PRACTICING DAILY GRATITUDE?

You are probably thinking, *we already discussed being grateful.* True. – We did. What we didn't discuss is the power of intention in your daily gratitude. As an exercise.

This exercise won't make you break a sweat either! Get yourself a pad of paper, notebook, a journal (if you need a recommendation, I have a published self-empowerment journal available on Amazon) something that you can write in daily. Yes, daily!

At the end of each day, all you have to do is write out what you are grateful for. Big or small.

Example: *I am grateful for the hummingbird that stopped by my feeder while I was enjoying my morning coffee. I am grateful for Chaka Khan and the song "I Am Every Woman" because I may or may not have played it on repeat to help me focus while writing this book. I am grateful to my hairstylist Sarah for fitting me at the last minute for a cut and color because I needed these bangsssss, and I needed them now! I am grateful for my husband bringing me Starbucks, always. I am grateful for my life, for opportunity, for grace, and for TikTok!*

The day has been full of trials and distractions. SO. MANY. DISTRACTIONS. Don't get caught up there. Focus on the blessings. Writing daily about all you are thankful for, it will change your perspective. You will be more aware of your blessings and how frequently they show up for you! Keep counting. Blessings AND stairs!

#12 PRIOR PREPARATION PREVENTS POOR PERFORMANCE.

ARE YOU RUNNING THE DAYS? OR ARE THE DAYS RUNNING YOU?

Gear check! At this point of the climb, you should have added a water bottle and a journal to your belongings. You haven't yet? Get it together!

You cannot, like CANNOT, make progress and perform to your full potential without preparing yourself in advance. You must have the plan and the equipment necessary to carry it through to completion. Otherwise, what is the point?

Do you have a hobby? I love to create things. Could be a shirt, a painting, turning half of the storage room in the basement into a gym – because aesthetics. Whatever project my mind conceives, I have to sit and plan it out. Like the gym. My husband and I had to build a wall to cut the room in half. We had to decide what we were going to put on the walls since it was just studs at the time. We decided to go with the pallet board look that was trending and that we would make it out of plywood. We had to make sure we had enough plywood, cut it into the right number of "boards," several colors of stain to achieve the right look, and plan the layout so that the correct variation was accomplished. Not preparing in advance could have resulted in not having enough boards or worse, the walls looking patterned not natural.

Whatever you are doing, be prepared. Prepared to perform. Prepared to win. Not preparing is a sure bet on failing.

#13 REST IS NECESSARY.

WHEN WAS THE LAST TIME YOU TOOK A BREAK?

You've been working so hard at life and of course, climbing these stairs. You definitely deserve a break! Let's relax for a bit.

Real rest though. Not sit down and scroll your favorite social media platform for hours. I am referring to the type of rest that relaxes your mind. To unplug. Downtime.

Relaxation is not the same for everyone, so I can't write a simple prescription for you. It's important to note –

relaxation isn't the activity itself; it is the end result. I suggest trying different activities such as:

Yoga.
Napping.
Meditation.
Taking a bath.
Getting a massage.

The key here is paying attention to how you feel after your chosen activity. Ask yourself a few questions: *Do I feel at peace? Do I feel a sense of calm? Do I feel grounded? Do I feel stable?* Those are the desired outcomes. That is how you will know that you have achieved relaxation.

You can't keep climbing if you're mentally and physically running on fumes. That could result in serious injury. DO NOT ATTEMPT.

14 EMOTIONS ARE TEMPORARY, CHOICES ARE NOT.

ARE YOU GETTING LOST IN YOUR FEELINGS?

I certainly hope that it isn't that you are experiencing feelings of guilt since you took a break. We can't have any of that!

I ask from experience. When I would find myself lost in my feelings, it was always because I had made myself feel guilty. Not because I had done anything wrong, I was instead internally beating myself up for not doing more.

I was abandoned by my mother at birth. I was raised by my father who was a former Marine. I was the middle child of 7 siblings. I always felt like I had to do the most. Be the most. Just to be seen or heard. Whenever I allowed myself grace, I felt guilty for it. Then I would get so lost in the guilt that I would make unhealthy choices in an attempt to seek the praise (or attention) of others.

Have you ever looked at a choice you made and wondered what you were thinking? You weren't. Your emotions and/or guilt were in control. We have to get better at making decisions based on what fills our hearts. What makes us feel good and proud and the happiest, regardless of what others might think or say.

This is your journey. You are not living for the benefit of others. You are climbing these stairs to make yourself stronger and healthier. To fulfill your own potential. To be proud of yourself. Make your choices based on that, not on the emotional guilt that comes with trying to please others.

#15 NO COMPARISON.

ARE YOU TRYING TO BE SOMEONE ELSE?

This is a serious question. Today more than ever, there is so much pressure on how you look and how you sound and what you do, how much you've accomplished…

We get so caught up in comparison that we lose our true, authentic selves.

Recently, I have gotten caught up in the task of creating a big social media presence. I've been working on building my second business, empowerment coaching. Unlike my insurance agency, that business is less revolved around my geographic community and more about reaching as far and as wide as possible. To help as many people as I can. So, it seems necessary.

I get reminded from every angle: my business coach, web designer, and other business owners in my circle – it's Instagram this and Facebook that. You have to create this, and you have to post that. And the worst one, "...that could've been content. Why didn't you record that?" ~~But~~ when I get on whichever platform, I catch myself comparing me, to what I see; *tell myself I am not smart enough, pretty enough, funny enough, I don't dress like her...*

This is some toxic behavior. We must not engage in comparison. The same light we see in others shines inside us too! The world needs us to show up!

No comparison! No excuses! *Shut the but up!®* and keep climbing!

#16 TAKE OWNERSHIP.

IN ALL REALITY, CAN YOU CONTROL ANYTHING OTHER THAN YOURSELF?

When was it lost on people that they are in control of their own reality? Don't like your life? Change it! And whatever you do, please don't blame someone else.

This might be a trigger of mine; it's certainly one of my pet peeves. People blaming other people for how their lives have turned out. I just can't comprehend it.

Hear me out.

My dad was an alcoholic – is that an excuse for me to become one also? My drug-addicted mother left me in a hospital when I was born – would that have given me an excuse to do the same when I ended up having my first child at 17? My stepmother stayed with my dad even though he was abusive – did that give me an excuse to stay in an abusive marriage? I had a kid at 17 – would that have been an excuse to give him up? I had a kid at 17 – would that have been an excuse to not graduate high school?

I could go on and on with this one, ~~but~~ I won't. I never wanted to be a victim. I chose to survive. I chose not to blame. I decided to know better and do better. I decided to never stop pushing and growing. I decided to strive for greatness and be an example that my children would be proud of.

Shut the but up!® and take ownership. Hold yourself accountable for everything in your life. This is your stairway; you are responsible for getting to the top!

#17 DO THE THING.

WHAT IS HOLDING YOU BACK?

We have already determined that living for other people is not the move. Nor is living in a state of comparison or placing blame.

Taking this into account, if you still have something you know you need to do, want to do, your heart overflows whenever you think about it because it is the one thing that brings you joy...why haven't you done it yet?! Maybe you just need this push.

Storytime! I spent the last 6 1/2 years recruiting people into an industry that isn't for everybody. I was great at selling "the dream." ~~But~~ when people didn't work out, I would blame myself.

I didn't consider the fact that my success in the insurance business was directly related to my WHY. That not everyone I recruited would have a WHY attached to that specific industry, that would motivate and inspire them to keep pushing. I didn't consider that my purpose for coaching others was greater than the confines of what success looked like in a specific industry.

I genuinely wanted those working with me to realize their full potential, their gift, their purpose – no matter what direction that would take them. When I woke up to that, I knew what I needed to do to fulfill my heart's desire. I knew then that I needed to write this book. I also knew that I needed to stop recruiting people into my business and instead start coaching anyone and everyone into following their own WHY, the reason they must do the thing. I did the thing, I stepped down out of my leadership role and opened myself up to empowerment coaching.

Doing the thing, whatever it is, will bring you an indescribable level of pride, a sense of peace like you've never experienced, an excitement that will make your heart skip a beat. I promise.

Decide to *shut the but up!®*, do the thing, just like you decided to take the stairs!

#18 DO IT SCARED.

WHAT ARE YOU REALLY AFRAID OF?

If you are anything like me – the answer is spiders, snakes, and being recorded on video. Yes, being on camera to me is on the same level as sitting in a room FULL of wild boa constrictors!

Until a few weeks ago. Until then, I avoided it at all costs. Flat out refusal. Hard NO. I was called out on it. I was asked, how can I be a creator, write a book like *Shut The But Up!*® if I can't practice what I preach...oh boy. Here we go with the challenges. I am not one to back down from a challenge! And now, the world has me on video.

I made a post on IG while they were setting up the cameras for the interview. The whole time I thought I was going to puke! The image I posted was a picture of myself with a quote that shared, "Do the thing! Whatever it is...even if you have to do it scared!"

I was BIG scared at that exact moment. My caption went on to explain my fear of video and the importance of facing your fear. Part of the caption included me saying, "Most often the things we need to do the most are the things we are scared to do! We always find a way to insert the '~~BUT~~' before the excuses."

Growth doesn't come from comfort zones! You need to do the thing. Even if you have to do it scared!

#19 STARTING IS THE HARDEST PART.

WHAT IS YOUR FIRST MOVE?

Think of it as a game of chess. To win, you have to make a move. To make a move you have to have knowledge. The knowledge is gained by learning lessons along the way. Your life is each and every one of the pieces carefully moved.

I am not a chess player. Now that I think about it, I don't think that I have ever even tried to play. ~~But~~ I watched *The Queen's Gambit*. Got slightly obsessed with it, I might add. I'd like to think that if I ever do try to play, I could be one of the best chess players ever.

No matter what sport or game you are into, you can find a fitting analogy and compare plays to the moves in life. The quality of the plays will impact how long it takes to finish. Also, the quality of the plays will determine who wins and who loses.

Another consideration is the players. Let's talk basketball, talk wins. Think of the contributions of the starters vs. those on the bench...if I was a starter and was on the court a majority of the game and you never got off the bench. Have we both put forth the same effort that brought our team the win? Would each of us feel the same level of satisfaction? I doubt it.

To get where you want to go, you have to start. You must make your moves. Strategically. Go get what is yours! We aren't climbing these stairs for nothing!

#20 YOU CAN DO HARD THINGS.

DO YOU BELIEVE IN YOURSELF?

This would all be pretty pointless if you didn't believe in yourself. Honestly, I don't think that a person who didn't believe in their own potential would even be reading this book. So, there's that.

I believe in you. I believe in everyone. I believe that anyone can do anything if they set their mind to it and decide they truly want it.

I have found, more times than I would like to admit, that I have wanted success for people more than they wanted it for themselves. They could be on the brink of achieving, more than they hadn't even imagined, and would walk away because it got a little hard. I still haven't quite figured that out yet. Is that because I just can't identify with that mindset? We will probably never know.

We have established that you believe in yourself, you have to or you wouldn't be on this page. You know you are full of untapped potential. We know that you are going to do the thing, even if you have to do it scared!

WARNING: Once you get over the fear and get started, it might seem easy – I need you to be ready for what happens when the adrenaline wears off – It will get hard. You will want to quit. This is normal. <u>Do not give up</u>.

When it gets hard – *shut the but up!®*, drink the water, take the rest and keep climbing! The reward is up there!

#21 CHOOSE YOUR HARD.

FAILURE OR SUCCESS, WHICH DO YOU CHOOSE?

It's the winning for me. It's the overcoming all the obstacles and being proud of myself for me. It is the setting an example for my children, for other women, other business owners for me.

The first time I contemplated that question I think it was posed in the form of money. Something like being poor is hard and being rich is hard – choose your hard. I have been both. I have had success and failures. I can attest that they are both hard.

I would like to have it on record that success is not even about the money for me, anymore. There was a time where I thought that having more money would mean fewer problems; that isn't true. Being successful has come with a set of troubles I couldn't have prepared for...well that might not be completely true; my aunt warned me about it when I was in my teens.

Let me leave out the story time and just give a piece of personal advice: do not, I repeat **do not** ever mix family (parents, siblings, cousins...) and business or family and finance. SMH. No matter how pure and genuine your intentions are, as soon as the handouts stop, you will be the villain. Spare yourself. Don't do it.

The choice is really about choosing to keep striving for success even if you fail a million times. I know you well enough by now to know that you won't choose to quit because of a failure or two. You will make your moves and stick it out, even when it gets hard. You will also continue to climb these stairs like a soldier, and we will celebrate together at the top!

#22 IF YOU START, YOU FINISH.

WILL YOU KEEP GOING?

Nothing comes from quitting. If you found the strength to overcome your fear and start, why doubt your ability to find the same strength to keep going?

I warned you that it would be hard. That it wouldn't be all sunshine and rainbows. I believe in tough love. I am not a fan of participation trophies. When you start something, you see it through to the end.

When I made it known that I was going to open myself up to the public for empowerment coaching, when I made it known that I was writing this book and launching it on my 40th birthday, when I made it known that I was starting a women's empowerment organization for community women business owners, when I made it known that I was going to start a nonprofit to mentor high school junior and senior girls that wanted to go into business instead of college...I did so intentionally. I knew that once I put it out into the world, I had to see it through. I knew that even when it got tough, I couldn't give up because too many people knew about it, and I ain't no quitter!

If you start something you have to see it through. I know that every person reading this book is on a different journey. Each person is fighting a different battle. One thing is for certain, whatever it is... these stairs apply. Whatever it is, you can *shut the but up!®* and see it through. You will be so proud of yourself when you get to the top! Just keep going!

#23 ALWAYS, ALWAYS TRY AGAIN.

DID YOU GIVE UP THAT EASILY?

I know you did not! There is no way that you made it up this far just to quit as soon as you stubbed your little toe!

The one thing that I have always tried to remind people (and myself) when they fumble, is that when you feel like quitting it is most important to remember why you started. If you can attach a reason to why you began, you can apply that same reasoning to why you must keep going. It becomes mandatory.

Quitting is easier, I get it. Just like frowning – or so we've been told...~~but~~ it isn't good for your mental health. It's filling yourself up with bad fuel. A lifetime of the unknown. Let me just tell you now so you don't have to find out the hard way later- the what-ifs are suffocating. Do you want that? No? Good.

Here is what you are going to do:

Reset.
Readjust.
Refocus.
Restart.

Anything worth doing, anything worth having, is not going to be easy. ~~But~~ you are built for this. You can push through. Trust the process, keep the faith, stay prepared, and see it through to the end (yes, no matter how many times you have to reset). Winners fail until they succeed, so climb on!

#24 EFFORT IS A DIRECT REFLECTION OF INTEREST.

ARE YOU MAKING A GENUINE EFFORT?

Avoid people who half-ass their way through life. Make certain you're not the person, the type I'd advise others to stay away from.

We have no time for anything half-ass. Say NO to giving or receiving half-ass effort, half-ass love, or half-ass energy.

I was feeling particularly spicy the other day. Agitated by something I saw that made me think of all the half-ass people who have been comfortable in taking advantage of my full-ass heart. In response, I made a passive-aggressive post on social media. No, I do not have any regrets, I think it was quite brilliant. Picture an old-fashioned recipe card- the one your grandma would've written her apple pie recipe on, the recipe everyone always asked for, the one she would never share because it was her secret. That was the vibe of my post.

PIE RECIPE

You wanted a piece of the pie.
I wanted to give you the recipe.
We are not the same.

Stay clear of those that are not making a genuine effort in their own lives. If they are sitting around waiting for everyone else to share their pie, they aren't worth you sharing a slice! If you keep giving away all your slices, you are never going to be able to enjoy the fruits of your own labor. Enjoy your own pie and keep climbing!

#25 COURAGE OVER COMFORT.

ARE YOU WILLING TO STEP AWAY FROM YOUR COMFORT ZONE?

That last stair was an eye-opener, right? Made you think of some situations that you maybe hadn't wanted to face? It's hard to accept that there are people that will stick around just for what they can get out of you without matching your effort.

Are you willing to step away from what and who is nothing more than comfortable to you so that you can continue to grow and reach your full potential?

There is a certain level of courage that will be required of you. Choosing courage over what is comfortable is about being true to yourself. It is the ultimate test of vulnerability and willingness to do something with no guarantees.

Stepping away from a miserable J.O.B. that provides a "guaranteed" paycheck every two weeks to go into business for yourself is choosing courage over comfort. Leaving an abusive relationship, walking away from toxic family members, cutting ties with those conditional friendships, all of that is choosing courage over comfort. Giving up your favorite x2 daily latte from Starbucks is also choosing courage over comfort. I might not recommend that last one for myself (yet), ~~but~~ this journey is all about you, Boo!

Shut the but up!® and choose you. Choose courage over comfort. I know at this point in the climb you have muscles burning that you haven't felt in a long time, or maybe never. ~~But~~ that means they're working hard! Heads up, you only have 86 steps to go!

#26 FEAR IS THE ROOT OF YOUR PROBLEMS.

DO YOU KNOW WHAT FEAR STANDS FOR?

Forget Everything And Run.
or
Face Everything And Rise.

The choice is yours.

I am sure you thought that I would say "False Evidence Appearing Real" – that works too. Let's break down your choices.

You know what you want to do and you know you should do it scared. Hopefully, you've started by now and chosen courage over comfort. I know that it is hard and we are all wired with the fight or flight response.

Flight is choosing fear. Forget-everything-and-run is choosing fear. Not because there is actual evidence that what you are doing isn't going to work – it's because you don't want to fight through the hard to get to the other side.

Fight is choosing you. Face-everything-and-rise is choosing you. It's choosing to fight through the hard because the reward is much greater than the risk.

We all have the fight inside of us, ~~but~~ you have to ask yourself here – *how badly do you want it?* Whatever your journey is right now, what is it worth to you to fight through the hard and uncomfortable? Just like climbing these stairs. It is hard work, ~~but~~ once you get to the top you will be so proud of how hard you pushed yourself!

#27 FREE YOUR MIND.

WHY ARE YOU STILL DWELLING ON IT?

You decided to fight through the hard! I am so proud of you for that. Great choice! Only one potential problem – are you fixated on what could go wrong instead of what could go right. I can relate.

Earlier in the book, I shared that I left my J.O.B. and started an insurance business with literally NO knowledge or experience. What I have not previously shared was that I made like $40,000 in my first six weeks. I was high on confidence. My WHY was strong. There was no space in my head for thinking about what could go wrong, so everything was going right!

Then a blizzard-like winter storm hit our area, and I was stuck in the house for close to two weeks. I began to feel deflated because I wasn't out generating business, and I started to overthink, to stress about how long this downtime was going to last. *Were all of my prospects going to die out?* Sure enough, since I put it in the universe, I started getting calls canceling meetings because they changed their mind or decided it was bad timing.

I have proof of what the results look like when your mind is free and I also know what it looks like when you are so consumed by what could go wrong. What you put out will come to you. *Shut the but up!®*, free your mind and stay confident. You will win! Keep climbing!

#28 IF YOU LACK OPTIMISM…

ARE YOU MORE FOCUSED ON WHAT COULD GO WRONG INSTEAD OF WHAT COULD GO RIGHT?

It's understandable if you have never been here before. There are some important daily practices that will help strengthen your optimism muscle and keep you going!

Remember why you started. In the beginning of something new and unfamiliar, it is almost second nature to be on alert and look for what could go wrong. The unfortunate side effect of doing so is that you will likely look for the wrong and find it. Always remind yourself why you started!

Find your inner coach, your inner cheerleader, and your inner strategist. If there is something actually going wrong, work through it and find the solution (hint – the solution is not quitting)!

Reward yourself constantly. Celebrate all the wins, no matter how small they are. Some days, your only win might be that you didn't quit, and you should celebrate that ish.

Track your progress. Write in a journal every day. You will enjoy going back to that, reflecting on how far you have come, and all the obstacles that you faced along the way.

The goal is to stay focused on the positives You started – that is huge! Anything worth having or doing isn't going to be easy or it wouldn't be worth the fight!

Keep climbing!

#29 THOUGHTS BECOME THINGS.

DO YOU KNOW THE POWER OF YOUR IMAGINATION?

"Imagination is more important than knowledge. For knowledge is limited, whereas imagination embraces the entire world, stimulating progress, giving birth to evolution."
—Albert Einstein

If you can imagine something, you can create it. Whether it be tangible or intangible.

Are you old enough to know who Pee Wee Herman is? If not, google him. I remember watching his show as a kid and he had this box thing that he used to go into and make these video/picture phone calls. Back then we all thought it was the wildest thing and we would talk about how that could never come true – we were still talking on phones that were connected to the wall at that point. Now look at us- walking freely around the world, catching up with our friends near and far via FaceTime. Imagination.

I remember when I used to dream of the life that I live now. I remember when I left the crazy man, I had to move into this little, tiny rental house, and it was a struggle to pay all the bills, medical expenses, and take care of the kids. I remember that when I left the J.O.B. and started the insurance business, I wrote out what my life was going to look like, down to the smallest detail. When I say that I manifested ALL that I imagined and more – I mean it. I did it.

If you can imagine it, you can do it. There is a reason that vision is in your head. Bring it to life! You're making great progress, so keep going!

#30 WHAT YOU THINK ABOUT, YOU BRING ABOUT.

ARE YOU AWARE THAT YOUR REALITY IS A REFLECTION OF YOUR THOUGHTS?

If you tell the universe that you are a failure, the universe will agree. If you tell the universe that you are a winner, the universe will believe you.

The Law of Attraction is real.

I know this might be starting to sound redundant... ~~but~~ there's a good reason- this is usually the point in the journey where a lot of people quit. The point where it's too hard. It's too slow. It's inconsistent. This is also the part where if you keep going, the victory is just around the corner!

So, how does the Law of Attraction work? First, you have to believe in it. You know gravity is real right? Even though you can't see it? Same concept. Consciously or subconsciously, you are creating your reality every moment of every day.

Have you ever noticed that when you say, "I am having the worst day ever," it just gets worse? Conversely, have you experienced deciding that you are having the best day ever and everything goes accordingly? Law of Attraction. This is how you can control outcomes.

You think it, believe it, and act it into existence. The belief has to be genuine and consistent. The actions have to match your desired result. You can't say that you are going to have a *New York Times* Best Seller if you never write the book. If you believe you can make it to the top, keep going, you will get there!

#31 MAKE SURE THE STORY IN YOUR HEAD MATCHES YOUR ACTIONS.

ARE YOU LIVING ACCORDING TO YOUR DREAMS?

Basically, are the actions you are taking daily matching the story in your head of the life you want to be living, the goal you are trying to achieve, the moves you want to make?

Dreams do come true. I am living proof. ~~But~~ only if you take action.

The generations before you, the people around you, none of that has to determine the life you live. You are in control of how your story plays out. You have the power to make it match the visions in your head. Make sure that the actions you are taking daily are aligned with those visions.

I know I told you that what you put in the universe, the universe will always say yes to. I am reminding you once more because I don't want you to get it twisted. You can't tell the universe that you want a million dollars and you just lay on the couch watching tv waiting for it to fall from the sky. You have to make moves and show the universe that you really want it, that you are willing to put in the work to earn it. It is then that the universe will believe you and say yes.

Have you been writing in your journal daily? Did you document the end goal? If you haven't already, you need to add to that what actions you need to take to get there. Do daily check-ins with the activity and keep yourself on course! You got this!

#32 YOU'RE ONLY COMPETING WITH YOUR OWN POTENTIAL.

ARE YOU DOING WHAT IS NECESSARY TO BE BETTER THAN YOU WERE YESTERDAY?

We don't compare ourselves to others. We are only comparing our personal progress to our own potential. Which, may I remind you, is truly unlimited!

I was asked one time what I thought would be the one thing that would keep me from being successful. The answer was so simple – me. The person asking looked stunned, as if that was a thought she had never considered before. Unsatisfied with my answer, she proceeded to ask me what else might stand in my way. I am still unsure of the response that she was looking for. Did she want me to place possible blame elsewhere as if I don't control the environment I'm in or the type of people I surround myself with?

After where I came from? And what I've been through? I know there is nothing else that could possibly stop me. Death, maybe?

Our thoughts. Our choices. Our self-limiting beliefs. Our actions. The common denominator? Ourselves.

If you are not where you want to be in any area of your life, you have the power to *shut the but up!®* and change it. You are the only thing standing in your own way. Keep setting your bar higher and higher. You can get there!

#33 SHOW UP FOR YOURSELF.

WHAT HAVE YOU DONE TODAY THAT YOUR FUTURE SELF WILL THANK YOU FOR?

We need to be intentional in the way we are living. Every day. We must live with intention in order to keep aligned with the version of ourselves we are working towards and the goals we want to reach.

Showing up for yourself will look different for everyone. We are all in different places emotionally and mentally. You can figure out how you need to show up for yourself once you have a crystal-clear picture of who you are and where you are going, once you are committed to the life you desire to live.

If you battle with self-love and self-worth, you need to be intentional about your positive self-talk. I told you that I want to lose a few pounds. Honestly, I obsess over it. I have an auto-immune disease which I can thank for the unwanted inflammation and weight. I have been fighting with this for about six years or so now. And since this isn't the body I am used to living in, I haven't been very nice to it. Some days, when I am really frustrated with it, I have to work really hard not to talk down to myself.

Pay attention to the things you do and say and how they make you feel. How do they impact your growth? Are they part of your truth? Do (and say) the things that are true to where you are going. Be nice to yourself – you are all you have, and you are all you need to keep climbing!

#34 WHY NOT YOU?

SERIOUSLY, WHY NOT YOU?

Are you at the point in your journey where you are so excited about what you are doing and what you are going to accomplish that you start sharing with the people around you? Do you have people around you who are quick to tell you that you can't?

Typical. Sigh. People are really so predictable. You do know that they are only trying to talk you out of it because they aren't doing it themselves, right? They are only telling you that it's not possible because they don't believe it is possible for themselves. They don't believe in you because they do not believe in themselves. The naysayers have the most limited beliefs; it is pathetic. And we cannot find value in their opinions.

When I first got into the insurance business, there was this cruise to the Bahamas I had a chance to earn. It was through a production contest put on by one of the insurance carriers I represented. When they posted the contest, I immediately told one of my assigned "mentors" at the time that no matter what, I was going on that trip! Can you believe she flat out told me I wouldn't be able to, that there was no way I was going to qualify, that in all her years in the business, she hadn't ever made the cut so there was no way I would as a rookie.

The Oasis of the Seas is a beautiful cruise ship, and if you are ever in the Bahamas, don't buy a conch shell from a street vendor. You won't get it through customs.

Checkmate.

Tell me again, why not you? If you keep climbing the stairs, how can it not be you?

#35 BE HERE NOW.

ARE YOU PRESENT IN THE MOMENT?

One of the worst consequences of having those naysayers in your ear is that you can get lost in the past or feel anxiety for the future. Don't get caught up in that, live fully in each moment.

We have discussed awareness before, ~~but~~ it is relevant once again. Awareness can be the one thing that keeps you from going down the rabbit hole of what has already happened. You can't change it, so don't keep reliving it. Awareness can also help you put to rest the potential anxiety of what lies ahead.

If you fully live in each moment, like really in the moment, you will find yourself with more optimism, more happiness, more peace, more clarity. Your quality of life will improve overall. Because how many moments have you missed? How many opportunities have you lost when you weren't fully present?

Now that you are present, this is where you will be observant moment to moment in order to redirect your thoughts and actions. This is where you will elect intentional living on a consistent basis. You will practice mindfulness because you will never be lost "in your head."

With your new superpower of living in the moment, things will start to get much easier for you. You may have thought you reached your destination, ~~but~~ you haven't. Drink some water and keep climbing.

#36 SPEAK YOUR TRUTH.

ARE YOU STAYING TRUE TO YOURSELF?

Do you have the courage to speak your truth when it is necessary? Or are you trying to reduce yourself to fit in the minds of those around you?

What's that old saying? "Those who mind, don't matter and those who matter, don't mind." As you continue to grow, you will need to keep this priceless little nugget handy.

Around the wrong people speaking your truth can leave you feeling unsupported and unseen. ~~But~~ not speaking your truth will leave you feeling burdened by not being heard. They both feel bad, so why choose to dim your own light, or reduce your own greatness just to make others more comfortable? You are not living your life for the benefit of anyone else. Chances are, those that you do not feel safe or trust enough with your truth won't be around very much longer anyway. Even. If. They. Are. Family. Let me rephrase, especially if they are family.

Family. Man, they make it so hard. I have spent countless hours trying to crack the code on this one. The best I can come up with is that these are the people that had the raw and uncut version of where you came from, so they struggle most with accepting that you don't live there anymore.

Shut the but up!® and burn the bridge if you have to! Keep on climbing.

#37 YOUR VOICE MATTERS.

ARE YOU SPEAKING UP ABOUT THE THINGS THAT MATTER YET?

Regardless of how those naysayers make you feel, there is someone around you that needs to hear what you have to say. Your experience, your story, could make all the difference in their life.

I lost myself in the emotions attached to the value I let others put on my life. I let people who have not grown, not evolved in ANY measurable amount at all in their entire lives, mute me. I let them control how I felt and how I shared. I let people who did not live my life, control my narrative. Why? How could I let myself down like that?

I need you to use your voice. Listen, ~~but~~ then speak to be heard. Call out the elephants. Say the hard things. Speak the truth from a place of love. If you stick to this, not only will you be heard, ~~but~~ you will be heard by the people who truly need to hear what you have to say. Your voice will give you power. It will introduce you to a greater audience of people. It will open doors and put you on to possibilities that you couldn't even see before you started speaking.

You will again feel more peace than you've ever felt before. You won't be weighed down by missing the moment. Can you feel how much lighter you are getting? How much easier it feels going up each stair?

#38 STOP APOLOGIZING FOR WHO YOU ARE.

WHY ARE YOU STILL SO CONCERNED WITH THEIR OPINION?

Don't worry; it isn't just you. When you finally start to find your voice and begin speaking up in spaces where you would have stayed silent before, it is common to interject an "I'm sorry" in the sentence. Do not be sorry.

As soon as you say it, you have lessened the value of your statement. You are also reducing your own credibility by not being confident and trusting the strength of your stance.

This is another area to develop awareness in. Constant apologizing is a result of trauma and anxiety. Over-apologizing is known to be a coping mechanism, a way to manage your nervousness and fear of speaking up. Being conscious in the moment and aware of what you are saying – as you are saying it – will help you eliminate this habit. SN: Since it is 2021 and we all text constantly, there was a study I noticed recently that I need you to be aware of. It pointed out that the SMS version of over-apologizing (via text) is the addition of "lol" to messages. Messages where we are speaking our truth and want to protect ourselves emotionally, in case the reply we get is not the one we desire.

I know you may still be worried about not having certain people around even though you are now fully aware that they don't make you feel seen, heard, and valued. If this is still the case, you know it is not healthy, it's not how you want to be treated, and you know that you would never make people feel the same way. Those aren't your people. Your people are up at the top of the stairs waiting for you to join them!

#39 YOU ARE ENOUGH.

DO YOU KNOW YOUR WORTH?

Your value is not decreased based on other people's ability to see your worth. Your self-worth is determined by you! As the old adage goes, *"KNOW YOUR WORTH, THEN ADD TAX!"*

First, you need to know that NO ONE is ever going to value you more than you value yourself. Second, once you know your worth and what you bring to the table, you won't mind eating there alone.

Knowing your worth is going to make standing up for yourself and setting boundaries effortless! It will be easier to demand your worth in compensation. It will be easier to say no to the things you do not want to do. It will be easier to walk away from relationships where you can't be your authentic self. It will be easier to confidently speak your truth. It will be easier to invest in yourself and your future. It will be easier to trust yourself and the decisions you make.

This may be the point you start adding more self-love affirmations to your daily journal, writing statements like:

I AM ENOUGH.
I AM LOVED.
I AM IRREPLACEABLE.
I AM STRONG.
I AM WINNING.
I AM UNSTOPPABLE.

You are all these things and so much more! No more negative self-talk. You are loving yourself all day, everyday...flaws, faults, and all!

#40 NO ONE IS YOU.

DO YOU KNOW WHO YOU ARE YET?

*"Today you are YOU
That is truer than TRUE.
There is no one alive,
That is youer than YOU."*
–Dr. Seuss

Have you learned to enjoy time alone with yourself? Have you been asking yourself the hard questions – do your daily actions match the vision in your head? Are you aware of the things that you are truly passionate about and are you pursuing those things? Have you assessed the relationships you have and how they serve you?

Now that my kids are grown, I spend a lot more time reflecting. During these times, I often see flashes of times in my life where I "lived" on autopilot. Not realizing at the time that I wasn't living, and I wasn't me. I was just going through the motions. During those times, I forgot who I was. I didn't spend time with myself, in my imagination. I did not pursue my passions or the little things that brought me personal joy. And not even because I didn't have time, just because I forgot to.

Find yourself. Get to know who you are and do not let go of that person for anything. You bring quality and value to this world when you are living as your true authentic self. You can inspire others just by following your own path and purpose.

I am proud of how far you have climbed already, and I know the universe is also!

#41 DON'T EXPLAIN YOUR NO.

DO YOU CONSTANTLY TRY TO JUSTIFY YOUR "NO"?

We are loving ourselves, speaking our truths, and setting boundaries. And there may be people around us who can't understand why we are saying "no" to things we used to agree to.

It isn't for them to understand. Your life. Your rules. *Periodt.*

Steve Jobs has explained to us that *"Focusing is about saying no."* Take a moment to reflect. Think about how much of a distraction it is when we are always doing things that are inconvenient to us, that we really do not want to be doing, just to make other people happy. Until I was aware, I hadn't. I was aware of my frustration. I wasn't doing things out of love and joy; they were out of obligation. I was not being true to myself first. I didn't set boundaries on my time or my energy.

No more.

We are no longer people-pleasers; we are self-pleasers. That doesn't mean that we won't ever do things for others, that isn't the point. The point is that we will only do the things that we want to do. The things that will not leave us full of resentment.

I've experienced instant gratification by putting this into action. The users and abusers in my life let themselves out once there were boundaries in place. And yes, I let the door slam behind them. #Winning

Simplify your life. Lighten your load. Learn to say no. Keep calm and climb on!

#42 LESS IS MORE.

FEELING OVERWHELMED BY THE CLUTTER?

With all of your newfound awareness, you will find yourself feeling a little overwhelmed by clutter, by pretty much anything you find that takes up unnecessary space and energy.

If you answered yes to the question above, that is okay! It's actually a good thing! It means that you have been taking this journey seriously and really doing the work, so you are becoming more aware of the clutter. You know it's gotta go. And for that, you deserve a high five! Great job!

I often wonder how we got here. When did society begin to need to have all the things? We have to have the biggest and best house. More cars than we can drive. The newest gadgets and devices. We seek validation through friends, more followers and likes.

I, too, have fallen into the trap. The more wealth I built, the more I felt we needed to have. We do not need a 5000 sq ft house. We do not need two cars, a truck, a boat, and a motorcycle. We do not need the newest iPhone, iPad, Apple Watch, and AirPods every year on the day they are released. Our worth is not defined by these material objects.

The quality of person we are, is not measured by how many friends we have on Facebook, or followers on TikTok, Instagram, or Twitter. Not even by how big your circle of friends is in real life.

Reduce the clutter. Less really is more, and it will be much easier to carry what you truly need up the stairs!

#43 ELIMINATE THE UNNECESSARY.

WHEN IS THE LAST TIME YOU DETOXED?

...from the things and people that are in your way? Have you thought about the space they were taking up in your life and in your mind?

The burden of clutter can be debilitating. It can feel so heavy that it will stop you in your tracks and before you realize it, you've accumulated more and purged nothing. Let's clean up!

Time to take inventory. Make a list of the things and people in your space. How do they make you feel? Do they serve a purpose? Are they bringing about feelings of joy? Are they a reflection of your true self? Anything that isn't? Toss it.

Is that easier said than done? Yes, of course. We place value on other people and things because, at one point, we must've felt like we needed them. You might need to start small if this feels like too much of a task. If that is the case, then walk into a space and commit to eliminating 10 items. They don't have to be big, ~~but~~ commit to 10. Can you do that? I know you can. Once you do, just keep repeating the process until your space and your energy is clear, less cluttered.

Take notice of the way it makes you feel. How much easier it is to breathe. How much more peace and energy do you have. Just keep in mind not to replace what you removed. You've climbed so far, keep it up!

#44 ENERGY IS CURRENCY. SPEND IT WELL.

HOW ARE YOU SPENDING YOUR ENERGY? IS IT ADDING VALUE TO YOUR LIFE?

Let's assume you start each day with a tank of gas. You have the same amount of gas every day, but some things burn more fuel than others. Are you maximizing your fuel efficiency?

We can't be wasting gas. It is too expensive, and don't you know that we just went through a shortage?

That was crazy. Where you spend your attention and focus is where your energy flows.

So, someone annoyed you today. They didn't respect your boundaries, and you fed into it. You spent energy on them in the moment. When the episode was over, you spent time thinking about how annoying it was... more energy wasted. Then, you called someone to tell them what happened, more fuel wasted (not to mention you also used up someone else's fuel).

Everything we do uses energy. Physical work makes us feel tired the same way that intense mental work drains us to the point of fatigue. If you don't deplete your tank on the wrong things, you will have the energy needed to achieve the positive things you are working towards.

Consciously choosing how and where to spend your finite amount of energy will determine how successful you are in achieving your goals. *Shut the but up!®* and spend it well!

#45 MIND THE BUSINESS THAT PAYS YOU.

ARE YOU STILL INVESTING YOUR TIME AND ENERGY ON THINGS THAT DO NOT HAVE AN IMPACT ON YOUR LIFE?

If you are still struggling with this habit, I am going to recommend that you head back down to stair number 33. It is for your own good.

Do you need a list? Something to refer to as a reminder of the fuel wasters that most people spend their precious time and energy on that add absolutely zero value to their life? Keep reading!

Complaining
Whining
Grudges
Gossiping
People pleasing
Arguing
Not saying NO
Entertaining negative people
Self-criticism
Not being intentional
Comparisons to others
Worrying
Procrastinating
Random distractions
Not setting boundaries
Not being prepared

These are in no particular order, and there is definitely more we could add to this list, ~~but~~ I don't want to use up any additional precious space or our valuable energy.

You get the picture. Be mindful of how you spend your time and energy, always. Spending it minding your own and keep on climbing!

#46 SMALL FIGHTS ARE FOR SMALL FIGHTERS.

HAVE YOU LEFT THE PETTINESS BEHIND YET?

You are bigger and better than that. We aren't wasting energy and we aren't explaining ourselves, remember?

It has been over two years since I have spoken to certain members of my immediate "family." Don't judge me. That is what they tried to do, and see how far that got them?

You have a pretty clear picture of what my life looked like growing up, the obstacles that I had to overcome – the biggest being myself – as an adult. My immediate "family" didn't line up to give me handouts, a come up, or even solid advice for that matter. I had to figure it all out on my own. Because of that, I have made a ton of mistakes. I am not above admitting that. I can confidently say, though, that every time they needed help- financial assistance, opportunities, a place to live- they came to me, and I was willing and available to support. I gave even when I didn't have it to give. Not for applause, for love. Did I get that? No. As soon as the free rides were over, I was made the villain of their story. I was worthless to them. The last time was the last straw. I was no longer going to try and beg to be heard. Wasn't going to try to explain why the handouts stopped. They can gossip, call me whatever they want to. They are not worth my words. Not worth my energy.

You don't have extra fuel to spend on worthless fights. That pettiness is beneath you. You are bigger than that. You need to conserve your energy so that you can continue to climb these stairs.

#47 WAS THAT USEFUL?

DID THAT SERVE A PURPOSE?

We have spent enough time talking about others, let's take a moment to reflect on our own words and actions.

When I discovered this very intentional question, I felt like I had a whole new breakthrough! I don't just ask other people "Was that useful?" when they do or say things that are energy wasters like we discussed earlier, I also make it a point to ask myself.

If I find myself in my feelings, about to open my mouth to pick an argument with my husband about how he did such and such and it made me feel some kind of way, I first stop and ask myself if it's useful. In the grand scheme of things? Does it matter? Is it even real or just something I manufactured because I am not in the right headspace? Will I remember this in 5 years? In the next five minutes? If the answer is no, I shut myself up and keep it moving.

We all have to check ourselves. The better you get at this practice, the more second nature it will become to spend our energy well, and only spend it on useful thoughts and emotions.

You are getting so strong on this journey, now that you *shut the but up!®* and aren't wasting your fuel. The stairs are becoming almost effortless, right?

#48 SAY LESS.

HAVE YOU STARTED BITING YOUR TONGUE?

The awareness that you have now about how much you were saying that wasn't useful…shocking, right?

Was it more than you initially expected? For me, it was. I began to notice how many conversations I was guilty of wasting my precious time by participating in…all the pointless back and forth.

Much like most industries, the insurance industry is gossipy and political. At the height of my career, my phone would ring constantly. "Did you see this? Did you hear about that? Can you believe he did that?" I was all the way invested in these conversations. I wanted to know who and what and why. I felt "important" because everyone was calling to give me the scoop. I never had to seek out the information; it always found its way to me, and that was perfect! Until it wasn't. It soon became exhausting. Overwhelming. I would be ridden with anxiety when I would see certain names pop up on my phone screen, quickly hitting the side button to silence the call. I didn't want to be rude, ~~but~~ I was busy.

Busy not engaging in another unnecessary conversation. I knew I had to withdraw. It was sucking the life out of me. So, I did.

I needed that. To *shut the but up!®* and start saying less. Engaging less. My life took on a new level of peace that helped me continue in my growth. I know it will do the same for you, too.

#49 NO ONE CARES.

ARE YOU SACRIFICING YOURSELF FOR OTHERS?

You know what else I learned when I fell back and started saying less. No one cares. Sorry to break it to you, ~~but~~ no one cares.

What happens when you don't answer the phone and engage? They just call someone else. They will call around until they find someone who, just like them, places no value on their energy and time, someone ready and willing to waste time gossiping.

Another warning- now that you are "acting different," don't be surprised when you are added to the list of topics they gossip about. And no, you aren't going to call them out on it, remember? We don't explain or justify our decisions for anyone, anymore.

Seriously. When I say no one cares, here is a way to fact check: How many people have come in AND out of your life? People that, at one point, you were damn near attached to at the hip? I am talking about romantic partners, friends, co-workers, family members, even the neighbor across the street. People that you thought, *"Oh, you are my best friend forever & always"* or *"I love you so much. I couldn't live without you."* Or what about the person you promised to *"love, honor, and cherish until death do us part"*?

How many of them are gone from your life (and I don't mean parted by death)?

See, no one cares. Do you, Boo! Keep climbing!

#50 YOU AIN'T THE ONLY ONE.

DID YOU ACTUALLY THINK YOU WERE?

Matter of fact, you aren't the first, and you absolutely won't be the last.

I know that is a pretty bold statement to make. ~~But~~ it is a fact. Literally, there is nothing about any of our struggles that someone else can't respond to by saying, "Been there. Done that." Sorry, not sorry.

I am not saying this to reduce the validity of what you are going through, or to say that it isn't painful. Sit with the feelings. Feel each and every one of them in their entirety. Then, when you are ready to heal and move on, that's when you keep going. No one can put a timeframe on that ~~but~~ you.

Are you wondering what we are even talking about right now? Anything. Anything you want to apply it to, it applies.

Some of you, for example, might be sitting still with the realization that no one really cares. You may be trying to figure out how to move forward with this knowledge. The good news? No matter what you are sitting with at the moment, someone else has survived it, and you will too!

You have come too far to try and give up now. Process and move forward. We have more stairs to climb!

#51 IT WON'T LAST FOREVER.

HAS IT HIT YOU YET THAT EVERYTHING IS TEMPORARY?

Acceptance is half the battle. This is another realization that will help you use your energy wisely.

Emotions, thoughts, people, scenes, money, things…all temporary. Hold on, I just remembered another quote that I love by Elon Musk, let me find it…BRB:

"Do not ever attach yourself to a person, a place, a company, an organization, or a project."

*Attach yourself to a mission,
a calling, a purpose only.
That is how you keep your power
and your peace."*

I suppose if everyone knew and lived by this quote, there would be no reason for me to be writing this book. It is so true. Every word.

My hope for you is that you can continue to stay strong, that you remain true to yourself. Stop putting so much stock in other people, in things that won't last, and, instead, continue to live intentionally for you, to stay mindful of yourself, to invest your energy in all that makes you feel full and joyous.

Whatever pain is still lingering, always remember that "this too shall pass." Shake it off. I will see you at the next stair!

#52 DON'T RUSH.

WHY ARE YOU IN SUCH A HURRY?

Relax. This isn't a race. Things take time to grow. You already learned to trust the process. Sit down and enjoy the journey.

Hasn't anyone ever told you that good things take time or that anything worth having is worth waiting for? So, where did you leave your patience? Go get it!

You know how I told you that due to this book and the empowerment coaching, yadda yadda...that I knew I needed to start working on (i.e., learning how to do) social media: posting content, building a following, increasing engagement, all that jazz. Well, I have found that nothing tests your patience like trying to grow an audience of strangers when you have no clue what you are doing, you aren't very consistent with what you are doing, and you have like actual business to tend to so you don't have 24 hours a day to babysit these platforms. I list all of that to say my growth has been slow. I don't really do slow, so when I was meeting with my business coach last week, she posed a question: "Tammy, what if you did go viral? Are you prepared to go viral? Are you ready to go viral?" *Ahhhh.* Point taken.

As long as you are doing the right things- believing, taking action, it will happen. There is no reason to rush it. What is meant to be, will always be. Grass grows where you water it. Take time to absorb the scenery and enjoy the journey.

#53 EVERYTHING WORKS OUT.

WHY ARE YOU STILL WORRIED?

I promise. Everything works out.

I remember when my dear friend Bill told me this for the first time. It was at the height of the drama in 2012 that I told you about earlier in the book. I rebutted his philosophy so many times. At the time, I thought he was full of straight BS and just trying to ease my pain. It took a while, maybe two years or so before it dawned on me that he was right. Everything had worked out. And worked out better than I could have ever imagined it.

If it weren't for the crazy man experience, I would never have appreciated my current husband as much as I do. I am very intentional about telling him, about showing him how much I appreciate every part of him.

If it weren't for the accident and financial devastation, I would have never gone into a business that was so foreign to me, that would completely change my life.

If it weren't for all of the pain, the trials, the obstacles that I have had to fight through, I wouldn't have this story to share with you.

You can't have a testimony without going through the tests. *Shut the but up!®* and embrace them.

Everything works out. We are almost halfway up!

#54 TIME HEALS.

DO YOU NOTICE
THE HEALING?

It is not specifically the time itself. It is what you do with the time that actually heals.

This journey that we have been on has been all about cutting out excuses; finding ourselves, our purpose healing trauma, and setting boundaries…it has been hard ~~but~~ necessary work.

If you've been doing the work, then you will have noticed that the pain is subsiding. It is getting easier to manage your emotions and your energy. You have begun to find a new sense of peace and self-worth.

I am no doctor. I am not licensed in medicine or any type of natural healing. I am giving you these steps as advice based on my real-life experiences and the results they have proven to bring. I am suggesting you apply these principles to your own journey and watch how your life improves because of them. Watch how you begin to heal.

None of us have deserved to endure what we have experienced. I have been on a mission to heal for as long as I can remember and, quite frankly, the hundreds and hundreds of books I've read have all been missing something…so here I am, writing this book. For me. For you. For everyone.

I am proud of us. I am proud of those who want to heal, who refuse to be a victim, those who want a better life, who want to live with purpose. Shall we do a victory dance now? We are celebrating all the wins!

#55 DIAMONDS ARE FORMED UNDER PRESSURE.

HAS IT ALL BEEN FEELING TOO HEAVY LATELY?

That probably means this process is working. No pressure, no diamond. No struggle, no strength.

1998. It was almost the end of my junior year of high school. I had like four part-time jobs and big dreams. I knew as soon as I graduated, I was getting the hell out of the small town I'd grown up in, and I was going to live in NYC. I planned on going to college there and working for a big-time fashion magazine. ~~But~~ I hadn't planned on getting pregnant. I remember the thoughts and feelings like it was yesterday. *No, no, nooooooooo! This cannot be happening. Not to me. My father is going to kill me. My life is over. There go my dreams. All for what, one bad decision with a guy I had just dumped because he said he was too old to go to the prom with me. O.M.G.*

I am here to tell the story, so you all know that my father didn't kill me. Everyone around me was telling me how my life was over. They had so much to say: "Have an abortion. You won't be able to do anything with your life. You are worthless, a statistic." On and on. Nine months later, I delivered a healthy and perfect baby boy. A few months after that, I graduated (on time) and from that point on I have worked my butt off to be the best damn mother and example I could be for him.

Was it easy, no. Would I trade it for anything, never! The pressure at times felt like a ton of bricks for sure, but I wouldn't be the shiny diamond I am if it wasn't for all of that pressure!

We get our strength from our struggles. We may not enjoy it; it may not always be pretty. ~~But~~ it does the trick. Keep climbing because you got this!

#56 NOTHING CHANGES IF NOTHING CHANGES.

ARE YOU WILLING TO MAKE THE CHANGES?

Doing the same things over and over and expecting different results is the definition of insanity.

What else should we call it when you continue the same habits and behaviors even though you have full knowledge that nothing is going to change if nothing about your process changes?

Are you still saying yes when you want to say no? Are you still surrounding yourself with people that suck the life out of you with their negativity? Are you still apologizing when you speak your truth? Stop. It. Now. You know what is best for you. You know the people that give you life and the people that take it from you. You know what you are capable of and what you have to do to get where you want to go.

There were certain people that always wanted me to give grace to my father for being an alcoholic because alcoholism is a "disease." No, what I fight every day is a disease (AGS, Lyme, Crohn's) not the result of a conscious and sober decision that I made. It happened to me, not because of me. If this triggers you, sorry not sorry. Alcoholism is a choice, not a disease, and you will not change my mind.

You make a choice every moment. The choices you make impact all that follows. *Shut the but up!®* and make better choices, and you will have an easier climb and a better life.

#57 FAIL FORWARD.

ARE YOU LEARNING OR REPEATING?

~~But~~ *Tammy, I am only human. I am not perfect.* You're right, there is no such thing as perfect. Are you learning though?

I've said it before and I will say it again: know better, do better. Every moment, you make a choice. That choice impacts what follows. When you make a bad choice, do you think *oh well* and keep repeating it? Or are you self-aware and reflecting on how an alternate choice would have served you better, provided you with a more desired outcome?

Let's pretend I hired you to set appointments for me. The appointments are for me to present our solutions to potential new clients. You have creative freedom to do this however you'd like – phone calls, emails, social media, snail mail... I don't care about the method, just the end result. This position would be commission only, so you determine your paycheck by the work you put in. If you'd tried one method for a while and it didn't bring any results, would you keep doing that or would you try something new? Everyone around you is setting appointments. Everyone around you is making money. Would you decide to self-reflect? Would you take the initiative to review your activity (or most likely the lack thereof) and make changes to the choices you are making daily? Or would you place blame on me because you aren't making the money everyone else is making?

Shut the but up!®, learn to adjust and keep growing!

#58 DON'T EXPECT SIX-FIGURE RESULTS WITH MINIMUM WAGE WORK ETHIC.

ARE YOU ACTING YOUR WAGE?

Trigger warning. Everyone always wants to make all the money and have all the things, yet they don't want to do the work necessary to get it. Help me understand.

I probably don't need help understanding. We are in a world of participation trophies so, there's that.

The example I shared in step #57 was obviously a true story, a scenario that has happened a few times. There are people that I never thought I would not have in my life that I haven't seen or spoken to in years because of that exact scenario.

IMO – instead of how those situations ended, there were two alternative and more appropriate endings. The first would have been for them to just DO BETTER. Do the work they were hired to do and to the level they needed to make the income they wanted to make. The second would have been for them to maturely decide that they weren't cut out for the job and go find something else more fitting for them and the level of work they can handle.

I know you are wondering if the job was that hard. Absolutely not. You might also want to know if people in the aforementioned example made any money. Yes – more than they earned. The difference between successful people and people that aren't is simple. Successful people do the things that unsuccessful people are not willing to do.

#59 LIKE A BOSS.

ARE YOU OWNING IT LIKE A BOSS?

Or are you making excuses for yourself and placing the blame on everyone else?

For me, the worst part of stories like the one I shared above is that instead of it just not working out – which is totally ok (that business isn't for everyone and if it was the income potential would not be as great as it is) they had to be a victim. It had to be someone else's fault, had to be my fault. It was heartbreaking.

The things that have been said can't be taken back. The damage is done, and true colors have been exposed. What I didn't do was try to defend myself. I didn't fight to be heard. I didn't need to. I am a business owner, a professional, and I handle all of it like the freakin' boss that I am!

Anyone that has ever had to hire people has also lost people. It is what it is. We don't lose sleep over it. We can't. We have to keep running our businesses. Anyone that doesn't understand that and tries to make it personal – clearly has never run a business, so why entertain that kind of energy?

Make all your moves like a boss. *Shut the but up!®* like a boss. Keep your head up like a boss. A lion never loses sleep over the opinions of sheep. Keep climbing!

#60 MAKE A LIFE, NOT JUST A LIVING.

DO YOU FEEL FULFILLED?

They always say if you love what you do, you will never work a day in your life. I don't completely agree, ~~but~~ if you feel fulfilled it will feel less like work (and you will probably end up working harder than you ever have before).

The J.O.B. that I left before starting my insurance business was so very miserable. I was doing mortgage foreclosures/repossessions (mobile homes). It was the most depressing thing to listen to someone tell you about their battle with cancer then have to respond with a "Sorry to hear that, but if you don't make a payment, I have to take your home." Talk about the opposite of fulfilling!

When I started the insurance business, I was almost instantly successful. People would always ask, "How did you do it?"! It was easy, it was fulfilling. I had a why. I had been in a situation where I desperately could have used the type of benefits I was offering. I was protecting people from the same devastation I had experienced. With every new client, my heart was full. I had a sense of purpose. Finally!

Money is great, ~~but~~ it is just not enough. To live a full and satisfying life you have to live on purpose. You need to feel fulfilled in the work that you are doing.

Take a look at your life right now, what are you doing with it? Is it making your life full of passion and purpose or is it making (barely) a living (a paycheck)?

#61 BE UNAPOLOGETICALLY REAL.

ARE YOU PUTTING ON A MASK FOR THEM?

If there are people in your circle that you have to wear a mask for, they are not your people and that is not your circle.

I went through a phase where I would adjust myself, like a chameleon, based on the crowd of people I would be around. If they dressed one way, I would force myself to do the same. If they liked a certain kind of music, I would too. I was so worried about fitting in that I started to forget who I was. I wasn't being real; I was just blending in with my surroundings.

Who did that serve? I surely didn't benefit from it. Even though I was in their circle, I wasn't really in their circle. They didn't love me for me. They loved the reflection of themselves that I gave them.

Be true to yourself. Be unapologetically real. If you can't be that person where you are, remove yourself.

Your people will find you.

Go do what you enjoy. Whether it's for work or for play, go do the things you want to do. When you get there, talk to the strangers that are doing those things as well. Step up and step in. Be present. Be you.

Once you have connected with the right people, you will know. These people don't just stand on the side when you're struggling. They will climb down and help you up!

#62 YOU ARE WHAT YOU ATTRACT.

DO YOUR SURROUNDINGS MATCH WHERE YOU ARE GOING?

You attract what you are. Not what you want. If you want great, then be great.

Let me introduce more proof that the Law of Attraction is real! I am hopeful that you weren't actually doubting it, ~~but~~ just in case you were, I figured I should maybe provide more evidence.

I am sure you have heard the above phrase before, ~~but~~ have you considered its meaning? Most people tend to focus on the things that they want and when they don't happen, they want to know why nothing ever seems to work out for them. They question why they keep going through the same things.

Knowing what you want is simply not enough and it never will be. You attract what you are (currently) because you haven't worked within yourself. You attract what you are because you didn't (yet) learn from your mistakes. You attract what you are because you are (still) talking down to yourself. You attract what you are because your thoughts and actions are not in alignment with what you say you want.

I hate to break it to you. I don't like being the bearer of bad news. If you are stuck here, you need to go back down and start again closer to the beginning. You have missed some stairs along the way.

If you WANT great, then BE great!

#63 GREATER THE RISK, GREATER THE REWARD.

ARE YOU WILLING TO TAKE THE RISK?

Clearly, I'm not talking about driving while intoxicated or investing in some crazy Ponzi scheme.

Nothing worth having or worth doing is going to come easy. If it were, it wouldn't be so valuable now would it? It is going to be absolutely necessary to take a risk – it should be positive and planned – to achieve any level of greatness or success in life. This is why most people never get there. It is too risky. They are more attached to what they might lose than all that they could gain.

What could you lose? *Money.* That isn't a good enough excuse; you could lose that anyway. *Time.* Okay, time is one thing we can't afford to lose, ~~but~~ how could you lose it in this instance? If you are taking a risk at something great, you will definitely be learning and growing in the process, so is that really a loss of time? I don't think so. *Reputation.* We aren't talking about drinking and driving or Ponzi schemes or any other crooked activity remember, so that isn't a good excuse either.

Taking a risk is how you will find your greatness. Taking a risk will expose you to new challenges to reach new heights. Taking a risk will force you to become more creative and live outside the box.

Taking risks will help you *shut the but up!®*, determine what is really important and what you really want to achieve!

#64 THE SKY IS NOT THE LIMIT.

ARE YOU AWARE THAT THERE IS NO CAP ON YOUR SUCCESS?

They lied to you when they said that the sky was the limit. There are no limits to your potential. No limits to what can be accomplished. No limits when you decide to *shut the but up!®* and just go for it!

Once you have decided to take the risk, there are no limits to what you can accomplish, honestly.

When Thomas Edison created the lightbulb, do you think he cared if someone told him it wasn't possible? When Alexander Graham Bell invented the telephone do you think he was bothered if someone told him it wasn't feasible? If neither of them thought that there was a limit to what they could achieve based on the limits of what already existed, we shouldn't either.

The only limitations that exist are the ones that we put on ourselves.

Remember that cruise to the Bahamas that someone so assuredly told me I wouldn't qualify for? She had a self-limiting belief. I did not. I knew that I could accomplish whatever goals I set out for. I can proudly say that I have.

Whatever it is that you want to do, if it is in your head and in your heart, you can certainly make it your reality. No matter how big, how wild, how insane, how never-been-done, how never-even-heard-of-such-a thing it is.

Shut the but up!® There are no limits!

#65 TIME ISN'T REAL.

ARE YOU SPENDING IT WISELY?

At this moment, our present has already become our past. Today will soon turn into yesterday and we are constantly wishing we could figure out how to slow time down.

I read something once that described our perception of time when it passes too fast or too slow. Consider the instances where time passed too quickly- maybe an amazing weekend getaway you took spur of the moment to go visit a bestie you hadn't seen in years, a trip filled with memories, a moment you didn't want to end. Now, think about when time drags- like at work on a Wednesday, the third day in a row doing the same mundane tasks as every day prior, checking the clock constantly, the hand barely moving a minute or two. In both instances, "time" moved at the same speed. When you felt like it was slower, it is because you weren't making any memories.

Another thought regarding time. You never know how much you have left. Based on this knowledge, why allow fear to consume us to the point of wasting whatever time we have left? It seems obvious to me we need to take advantage of every single moment, to live life to its fullest, to live as our true selves.

Take risks. Make memories. You've come so far. Keep climbing!

#66 NEVER FORGET YOUR WHY.

WHAT IS YOUR DRIVING FORCE?

I am so excited right now! Talking about your WHY and driving forces is like my favorite thing everrrrrrrrrrrr! *Woohooooooo!*

Everyone has a WHY and a driving force; do you know what yours is? If you don't already, you will by the time you finish this page.

Your WHY is a constant. It is what will guide your heart and push you toward finding fulfillment in your life. It is your very own personal mission statement. The purpose behind your life's work, what you want to be known for.

Both defining your WHY and being aware of your driving force are essential. First, think of your source of motivation. When I was 17 and found out I was pregnant, giving my son a better life than I had was my driving force. He was my WHY. There could be no greater motivation. Now think of something you could talk about for an hour straight with passion and conviction. Something that, when you talk about it, you feel fulfilled because you are making a difference.

What is that? And why is that?

Now that you have identified it, does it make sense? There was an event in your life that made that important to you. The spectrum for this is so broad that it can only be defined on a deep, personal level. Over the years, this may change and that's okay. Be aware, be mindful of those instances, and adjust accordingly.

#67 PURPOSE ISN'T A DESTINATION.

DID YOU THINK YOU WERE GOING TO GET TO THE TOP AND STOP?

Life keeps moving and happening constantly, and as this happens, your purpose will change. This is a guarantee.

Don't be disappointed, this is what keeps life interesting – especially for those of us that are really living!

When I was 18, 19, and throughout my 20s, my kids were my purpose. They were my why, my driving force, my everything. Once in my 30s, my children were becoming semi-independent, and they needed me less. I hadn't lived for myself like ever, so I hadn't known any purpose outside of being a mother. Funny how the universe works, right? It decided to smack me so hard with another purpose that the result was 3 plates and 12 screws in my spine, about $38k in out-of-pocket medical expenses. I went into the supplemental insurance business after, and then my purpose became sharing my story in hopes of sparing others from experiencing the same. As my new purpose continued to grow, I began recruiting and training people into the business. This has led to an even greater purpose – empowering and coaching people everywhere to travel their own path, find their own gifts, and reach their greatest self.

Our purpose is constantly changing. You will never "arrive" and be finished. Stay woke and climb on!

#68 LIVE ON PURPOSE.

WHOSE MAP ARE YOU FOLLOWING?

Now that you have all the tools, are you going the right way?

I kinda want to list all the stairs you have taken right here to show you that you have all the tools you need already to live your life fully and completely on purpose. I won't, just know that I want to.

We are clear on the fact that we are living intentionally for ourselves. We know who we are. We know our WHY and our driving force. We have found our voice and our people. Now, it's time to share it.

Every day, you need to set your intentions on what that day will bring. You will need to establish your priorities and make sure to keep those in alignment with your mission.

Once you are living ON purpose, everything will begin to be super easy and almost effortless. You will see that everything just starts lining up and going your way.

You will be at peace.
You will be full of joy.
You will feel alive.

You have chosen to *shut the but up!®* You have chosen to take this climb on purpose, so I know you can make the choice to live on purpose as well!

#69 FALL IN LOVE WITH THE PROCESS.

ARE YOU TAKING THE TIME TO ENJOY IT?

I love me some Eric Thomas who said, *"Fall in love with the process, and the results will come!"*

Nobody:

Me: Did you know that I was supposed to be a volunteer at one of his events last year in DC, ~~but~~ COVID ruined that? *Insert eye roll*

I played Eric Thomas YouTube clips during *almost* every Monday Morning Meeting for my agents for a solid

5 years. It was his level of passion for me! What a great way to start the week!

"HOW BAD DO YOU WANT ITTTTTTTT?!?!" If you have never listened to one of his videos, you can grab a bookmark and go do that now. It is some seriously powerful stuff!

Moving on. Let's break down Eric's quote above:

In Love – A strong feeling of affection and concern.
Process – A series of particular actions or steps taken in order to achieve a particular end.

You need to have a strong feeling of affection and concern towards each action item and step taken in order to achieve your desired results. There is no way to be in love with the process and attempt to rush through it.

Slow down, take it all in, and make memories along the way. These stairs aren't going anywhere.

#70 VISUALIZE TO MATERIALIZE.

WHAT IS ON YOUR VISION BOARD?

You do have one, right? Because you need one.

A vision board, much like a journal, is a powerful tool to utilize as a daily reminder of your goals and dreams. Visualization of the life you are wanting to materialize is a highly effective mental exercise to improve your focus and keep your desires elevated.

There is a plethora of inspiration you can find on Google, and there are more styles and layout ideas than you could ever imagine.

When I build my vision board for the year, I focus on specific categories: Mental, Spiritual, Physical, and Financial. For each of those categories, I determine my next big goal and what are some smaller goals (action items) that I need to accomplish in order to achieve the wild goal. **Remember, we celebrate ALL the wins, big and small!** Make sure to include bold lettering, words of encouragement, pictures of specific things you want – make it as clear as possible so that when you look at it, you know exactly what you are working towards.

I like to review and update my board at the end of every month. That way, I can mark off what I have accomplished. This provides some self-validation and gives extra motivation for me to continue achieving my goals. Work on that vision board and then get back to climbing!

#71 BE INTENTIONAL.

ARE YOU SETTING YOUR DAILY INTENTIONS?

Setting and writing out your intentions each day will keep you focused, positive, and committed to your goals.

~~But~~ *I don't know what that means to set my intentions for the day...*

Ok. Have you ever (yes) had those days where it seemed like they just happened to you? When you set an intention for the day, you are taking control and manifesting what will come to you on that specific day. YOU are happening to the day, not the other way around. This will also keep you on track, support your staying mindful, and living on purpose. When it works for you, it will be yet another sign of how true and powerful the Law of Attraction really is.

When you write out your intentions, they will look something like "Today, I will..." or "I intend to..."

My intentions for today looked like this:

Today, I will make someone smile.
Today, I will laugh out loud.
I intend to be kind, even under pressure!

This technique paired with your vision board and daily gratitude? BOOM. Unstoppable! People aren't even going to recognize you by the time you get to the top! Keep climbing!

#72 YOU ARE WHAT YOU EAT.

HOW DID THAT FOOD MAKE YOU FEEL?

Don't get mad at me. I didn't make the rules. I am just the messenger!

I am not here to tell you to stop eating this and that you can't eat that. I am still the one that runs on Starbucks latte's all day, every day. However, I am also a forced vegan for the most part, with a side of Kosher organic pescatarian. I didn't really have a choice in the matter due to the AGS and all. (No, I absolutely cannot take up space in this book to explain the torturous mammalian allergy that I suffer from as a result of a tick bite, ugh.)

~~But~~ I am here to tell you that the foods you consume have everything to do with providing a solid foundation that is your body. You rely completely on your body to take you on this journey to purpose and greatness. If you don't take care of your temple, can you even be great?

If you struggle in this area, my first suggestion would be to analyze how you feel physically. Where are your areas of concern and focus? If you suffer from chronic inflammation, for instance, you probably want to add anti-inflammatory foods to your daily diet. If you have noticed that your eyesight is slowly declining, there are foods that are proven to improve it. Google can be your friend here. Just type in "foods that help with ..." and there you go! Or consult a nutritionist.

You have to provide the necessary nutrients to your body to keep it strong enough to continue the climb!

#73 DON'T BUY CHEAP PILLOWS.

DO YOU FEEL RESTED AND READY TO TAKE ON THE DAY?

This one is dedicated to you, Pally! #Throwback to approximately 2005. I was joking with my friend Aimee about writing a book on the rules of life. Well, here it is!

We have talked about the water, the food, and so, of course, we are going to cover a good night's sleep! You want to be great, right? In order to be great, you have to take care of the whole package, and quality sleep is a vital part of that.

I don't know about you, ~~but~~ there is zero chance I am getting good sleep if my pillow is crap! I know, there are so many different types of pillows- memory foam, down, microbeads, buckwheat hull, fake stuff, you name it. ~~But~~ this is important. Do you need it to be soft or firm? If you can't figure out what kind of pillow is most comfortable for you, go to your local mattress store and test them all out until you get that *ahh* effect!

Once you have your quality pillows and start getting that good sleep, you will notice that so many other areas of your day improve. A good night's sleep is proven to increase productivity and physical endurance; it boosts your mood and immune system, strengthens your heart, and prevents weight gain. It's a must!

Go get them good, GOOD pillows. Get that GOOD sleep and come back to keep climbing!

#74 GO OUTSIDE.

WHEN WAS THE LAST TIME YOU SPENT TIME IN NATURE?

Dear all things good in the world, do not tell me it was when you were like 12!

If my generation's parents did anything right, it was the amount of time they made us spend outdoors. I am pretty sure it was for selfish reasons; they probably didn't want us messing up the clean house or eating all the food or interrupting their "soaps". Whatever the reason, they sure got that part right!

There is a total hippie side of me that wants to tell you about standing in the grass and the dirt and grounding yourself with the universe. I assure you that it clears your energy and improves your healing journey. Spend time outdoors. Go for a walk. Be mindful of the gifts nature blesses us with like the trees, flowers, birds, the sky. This time is shown to boost your much-needed vitamin D levels (which the majority of us are deficient in, causing lower energy and chronic fatigue issues), improves vision, and brain function. If you don't want to go for a walk, just sit out there and read, set up a projector and watch a movie, have a picnic, or play with your dog.

Spend 30 minutes a day outdoors and watch your overall health begin to improve. You're welcome!

#75 BREATHE.

HAVE YOU PRACTICED BREATHWORK LATELY?

Slowly inhale through your nose and then pause. Then exhale slowly through your mouth. I just had some Lamaze flashbacks. Back to the task at hand, let's breathe.

People practice breath work to help them improve their mental, physical, and spiritual wellbeing. There are many different types of breath work that use different breathing techniques to achieve specific results. The one I seem to use the most is for increased energy.

Breathe in through the nose for 4 seconds. Hold your breath for 7 seconds. Exhale forcefully through the mouth, lips formed like you are blowing up a balloon, even making a whoosh sound, for 8 seconds. Repeat four times. Work towards completing eight reps per session.

Again, our friend Google is a great resource for finding breathing techniques, and the instructions are typically written for beginner use.

Breathe and climb on!

#76 DANCE IN THE RAIN.

CAN YOU STAND THE RAIN?

Our last few stairs were quite literal, but we are now headed back to the land of figurative speaking.

When New Edition released the song in 1988, it was your new jam. Did you know what it meant, or was it just a vibe? You know it was just a total vibe at the time.

Now, after decades of adulting, we appreciate the lyrics on a different level. Especially those of us who have lost people we love because they couldn't stand the rain. This isn't even exclusive to romantic partners.

We all have our share of friends and family members that got washed away in the storm. Should we have a moment of silence for them? Nah.

I want to talk about you though. Can you stand the rain? *"The storms will come/this we know for sure."* When you stumble across these obstacles are you going to give up and revert back to your old habits or are you going to break out all of your new tools and weather the storm? Tell me, can you weather a storm?

"Everyone loves sunny days," we know this, ~~but~~ if this level of greatness was guaranteed to be all sunshine and rainbows, do you think that it would be such important work?

You were born to be great, and you've made it this far, have your rainboots handy and keep going!

#77 SELF-CARE IS HOW YOU TAKE YOUR POWER BACK.

HOW DID YOU SHOW YOURSELF LOVE TODAY?

You do realize ALL of this is essentially self-care, right? I want to make sure you are consistently practicing all of your new skills.

How often do you go on TikTok and learn an "I was this many years old when I discovered _____" life hack that has blown your mind? How many times have you raved about it to anyone who will listen? Ever sworn it's a total game changer, that you will never live without this new badass trick, then the moment passes, and you never use it again?

That is how we are when we learn all of these new ways to take care of our mental, physical, and spiritual health. We don't make it a habit or routine, so it gets forgotten in the pile of all the other cool tricks we know.

You can't be great without making self-care a priority. You already know that it is more than lighting some candles and taking a bubble bath. You have to do the real work.

Make yourself a checklist, write it on the bathroom mirror. Stick Post-it notes all over the place. Set 15 different alarms on your phone. Whatever it takes for you to make taking care of YOU, your priority.

Shut the but up!®, put in the work and get great!

#78 FINE IS THE EQUIVALENT OF SETTLING.

HOW OFTEN DO YOU SAY "THAT'S FINE"?

Where are all my mamas at? You KNOW that when your kids ask you for something (ten hundred times) and you respond with "Fine," you really meant to say "No." Don't deny it.

We already discussed saying "**NO**" like twice and yet here we are. We aren't going to replace *yes* with *fine* in order to avoid *no*...that is what we definitely are not going to do.

Saying "fine" is a signature passive-aggressive phrase used to indirectly express anger. We are not about that energy or that life anymore. Get it together.

We say "NO" around here! No. no. no. no. no. no. no. no. no. no. no. Keep practicing if need be.

"No" is a whole sentence. It does not require explanation or justification. If you need a refresher, please refer back to # 41.

No.

No.

No.

No.

It feels so good to say. Short and sweet. To the point. Rolls right off the lips. You could even make a pretty sweet chant repeating it while you keep climbing.

#79 INDECISION IS A DECISION.

IS SAYING "NO" SO HARD THAT NOW YOU RESORT TO DECISION AVOIDANCE?

Are you afraid of saying "no"? And since "fine" is no longer a part of your vocabulary, add "maybe" to your list of words you no longer use as well. Maybe I should throw the whole book away? *J/k.*

We need to discuss indecision. Fear of making the wrong decision is the number one reason that people often feel hesitant to lead. Hesitating when given a choice, whether it's due to the possibility of failure or potential success, can come from a lack of trust in yourself, what you will do, that you will be able to handle it all.

I am not suggesting that you rush into all decisions; that is not responsible. You do need to go through the normal process of deciding. You should always gather as much information as you can, weigh the facts, determine pros and cons and then decide which way leans most in your favor.

When indecision becomes a problem is when you wait too long and your window of opportunity passes by. This causes a decision by default since you lost your choice in the matter completely.

Trust yourself. You have the skills to make good choices on this journey!

#80 BE STRONGER THAN YOUR EXCUSES.

WHY ARE YOU LYING TO YOURSELF?

I am beginning to wonder if I should go back to the beginning and interject more reminders to *shut the but up!®*?

It's always challenging as a leader to see more potential in people than they see in themselves. You sometimes want success for them more than they do. It can be emotionally exhausting when you have spent so much time and energy on one human being that cannot seem to get out of their own way long enough to realize all that they can accomplish.

Then, before you know it, they walk away from their dreams. They say that they just can't do it. They can't handle the rejections. They aren't comfortable with the inconsistency. They don't trust themselves enough to keep showing up. They need a safety net.

So many excuses and all of it is BS. They know it. I know it. You know it.

It got too hard is all it was. Too hard to do the self-work, the self-talk, the self-trust, the self-discipline. They'd rather walk back down the stairs than push through a few more cramps.

Are you going to give up too? Or are you going to do the work and stick it out? I sure hope you choose the latter.

#81 DISCIPLINE IS THE BRIDGE.

HOW ARE YOU KEEPING YOURSELF DISCIPLINED?

We are not talking about punishment. I am referring to the type of discipline that keeps you in line.

Oops. I mean aligned.

Discipline occurs when you use specific devices on a consistent basis to ensure that you are prioritizing tasks day in and day out that keep you doing the work required to achieve the greatness you desire. These self-enforced rules will keep your life in balance and running effectively and efficiently.

Having discipline in your life will force you to make small sacrifices now for the life you desire in the future. Today's habits and disciplines are directly linked to who you are in the future.

Learning how to *shut the but up!®* is discipline. Discipline is something you have to create, build, something you have to work at constantly. Just like your body and climbing these stairs, the more you work at it, the stronger and even easier it becomes.

#82 PEOPLE WITH SMALL MINDS CAN'T COMPREHEND BIG DREAMS.

ARE YOU OVERSHARING YOUR DREAMS ONLY TO HAVE PEOPLE MAKE YOU RECONSIDER?

Here we are again, entertaining the Negative Nancy's, the Petty Betty's, maybe even a Karen or two.

Kidding – or am I?

It's trending and funny. Lighten up. I am not kidding, though, about the fact that we are entertaining these people again when we were supposed to be clearing them out of our space. Don't worry. I am not surprised, and I know that this page isn't the end of the conversation.

As a matter of fact, we don't even have to get rid of everyone that can't see our vision. We just can't put the fate of our futures in their hands. These people probably don't have any ill intentions or bad energy, thank goodness. Their minds just aren't big enough. Are you picking up what I'm putting down?

Just because they cannot see the bigger picture, just because they could never believe in dreams as big as yours, does not mean that they aren't completely possible.

I would work on simply not oversharing at this point. If you are not around the circle of people that will feed into your energy, that will add hope and faith, don't share at all. It is not worth the unnecessary doubt that it could cause.

All you need is you to make it happen, and you got this!

#83 YOU DON'T NEED THEIR APPROVAL.

ARE YOU GOING TO LET THEM CONTROL YOUR DESTINY?

"Something remarkable happens when you truly stop seeking other people's approval. You automatically gain it. And find that others will then seek your approval."
–Unknown

It is my opinion that we are living in the heart of a society that is currently built on the approval of others. We need likes and followers to feel worthy and validated. We are even rating our own value by how much engagement we get on each social media post.

Imagine this: you are really feeling yourself today, and you post about it. You thought the picture was your best, even had the cute, witty caption to go with it. Out of your 500 friends on Facebook, you only get 5 likes. How does it make you feel? First, FB must be broken! You look fly AF! You start feeling down about yourself, maybe go so far as to delete the post because you feel embarrassed, ashamed, invalid, irrelevant, etc.

You are worthy (and super fly I might add) and you are oh so valuable! They just can't handle it!

Every time you place your own relevance in the hands of others, you will be disappointed. Without even realizing it, this will begin to negatively impact your freedom to create and achieve the life you desire.

You do not need anyone's approval – ever. You do you!

#84 THE CRITIC DOESN'T COUNT.

ARE YOU STILL LETTING THEM GET IN YOUR HEAD?

I said what I said.

In case you weren't already aware, this is a public service announcement: people that are outwardly critical of others are basically validating their OWN insecurities! They are telling you the negative perception they have of themselves!

We are already our own worst critics so when someone else is critical of us – our looks, lifestyle, habits, etc. – it can be really hard to handle.

Do not allow them in your head! Don't take it personally; people who are like this are most likely this way to everyone. Maybe they are clueless. Maybe they have good intentions and don't realize that they sound like big jerks.

Don't respond with anger – why would you give them that power over your emotions and energy?

Empathize with your critic. This will help you reduce the tension they've made you feel, and redirect that energy, and focus back on them.

Don't let them stop you! The critic doesn't count!

#85 CHECK YOUR CIRCLE.

ARE THEY ADDING VALUE?

If you allow people to make more withdrawals than deposits in your life, you will soon be out of balance and in the negative.

When you start living your life intentionally and on purpose, you will notice a change in the way that the people in your circle are treating you. Take note of the ones that seemed to like you better when you weren't speaking your truth, back when you had dimmed your own light. This is a friendly reminder that those are not your people!

Your people will not try to call you out on your change and growth in a negative way. They will not bring up your past mistakes and bad habits.

Your people will know that you don't live there anymore. Your people will celebrate your new heights; they'll most likely want to know how you did it, what you're doing, and they'll likely want to join you on the journey!

Your people WANT you to win and will be the ones clapping the loudest when you do!

As your life changes, so will your circle. As you continue to grow and evolve it will change many times over. Remembering this will make it that much easier to accept as it happens.

#86 ELEVATION REQUIRES SEPARATION.

WHO/WHAT DO YOU STILL NEED TO LET GO OF?

It's not personal; it's purposeful.

Once you've cut out the Negative Nancy's and Petty Betty's, you'll start seeking the activities that bring you joy with others that are doing the same. It's great progress. It frees up room to add people that not only have good vibes but are also on the same journey as you. This is where you will source your strength on the hardest of days. These are the people that will easily remind you of why you started in the first place because they are going the same way.

Surround yourself with people that also have dreams, desires, and the ambition to be the best version of themselves. They will help push you and keep you motivated so that you don't forget where you are going. This goes back to being intentional and mindful of the life you are living. Living on purpose.

While we're here, remember this: whatever that thing is that you have been holding on to and criticizing yourself over, that habit you have found so hard to break, the one that does not align with the picture of the life you are working towards? Take a step away from that. Today.

#87 THIS TOO SHALL PASS.

ARE YOU GOING TO LET IT BREAK YOU?

It might pass like a kidney stone, ~~but~~ it will pass! Nothing, bad nor good, lasts forever.

My husband and I were at a restaurant one night that we had never been to before. He had ordered this beautifully crusted sea bass that was so elegantly placed on top of a bed of a spinach risotto. I ordered shrimp & grits (yummy, that's my go-to meal if I ever see it on the menu).

The food comes, and it looks and smells amazing! Score! We began enjoying our meal and chatting. I think the majority of our conversation revolved around how impressed we were with the service, the ambiance, the cleanliness of the establishment, and how delicious our meals were. Our date night was a win and we couldn't be more delighted...until the Mr went in for his next bite only to find a hair (that didn't belong to him) on his plate, under his fish. *Waiter, check please!*

Talk about going from a high to a low.

I know this journey hasn't been easy, I know that you have had to learn how to *shut the but up!®*, how to let go of habits, people, and even things that once had made you feel comfortable and safe – only because that was your norm. Nothing worth having, including the life that you dream of living, is going to come easy.

Keep taking the steps. I promise it will be worth it!

#88 THERE IS PURPOSE IN YOUR PAIN.

HOW CAN YOU GROW FROM IT?

The reason for your struggle is the reward for enduring it all.

Have you ever started a new workout routine and, at first, it seems like a breeze because you are excited about it? ~~But~~ later, when you're less motivated, you feel like you got run over by the Amazon truck? Then you quit? I hate to break it to you – no pain no gain.

I really hope that I am not beginning to sound like a broken record with all of this. Human nature just tends to be pretty predictable, and the cycles seem to be pretty similar person to person.

Whenever I would hire a new insurance agent, I always gave them the same orientation. It included a high-level overview of what their career would look like with three slight variations. Eight out of ten would play out exactly as I had described, even down to that percentage (because I included that also). They would deny at first that they would struggle with a certain behavior or feeling (that was also included in my prediction) and then, when they decided that their path had come to the end, they were the ones saying that I was right.

I hate that part. People tend to start making the excuses again and quit right before the reward, ~~but~~ that isn't going to be you, is it?

#89 IF IT COMES, LET IT. IF IT LEAVES, LET IT.

ARE YOU FORCING IT?

Don't force pieces that don't fit. If there isn't flow, let it go.

We have all heard the saying that if you love something, let it go. If it comes back to you, it is yours forever. If it doesn't, then it was never meant to be.

What does that mean? This is one of the most fundamental rules of the universe. Especially if you are applying this to love. Love is not yours to own or to control. You are only intended to give it. If you truly love someone, you have to give them the freedom to choose to love you in return.

"Love is patient, love is kind. It does not envy, it does not boast, it is not proud. It does not dishonor others, it is not self-seeking, it is not easily angered, it keeps no record of wrongs. Love does not delight in evil ~~but~~ rejoices with the truth. It always protects, always trusts, always hopes, always perseveres."
-*1st Corinthians, Chapter 13, Verses 4-7*

Regardless of faith, this passage says it best and can be applied in all relationships and in all areas of your life. Don't force what isn't meant to be.

<u>Repeat after me:</u>

I do not chase.
I attract.
What is meant for me,
will find its way.

#90 MAKE PEACE WITH IT.

WHAT DO YOU NEED TO FORGIVE YOURSELF FOR?

You have forgiven them, ~~but~~ have you forgiven yourself?

Forgiveness isn't just about the forgiveness of others. We have to learn how to forgive ourselves. This is deeper than just putting the past behind you and moving forward. You have to be accepting of yourself, the choices you've made and why you made them. Give yourself grace knowing that when you made those decisions, you were doing the best you could with the knowledge you had at that time.

We all make mistakes. The good news is, they have already happened, there is nothing we can do to change them. There is a process of forgiveness that is important to go through so that you learn and don't repeat the same mistakes.

We need to first take responsibility and face what we've done. Then, let yourself feel the guilt. Good people make mistakes and it's healthy to feel bad for it. Now the next two steps tend to get left out of the process. Make amends with yourself. If you need to take action to rectify the situation, do so now. Lastly, grow from it. Knowing why you did what you did and what you learned will help you determine how you'll handle a similar situation in the future.

Was that like a ton of bricks lifted off of your shoulders or what?! Hallelujah!

#91 RESPECT IS GREATER THAN ATTENTION.

ARE YOU SACRIFICING FOR VALIDATION?

Choose respect. It lasts longer.

P!nk said it best: *"Once you figure out what respect tastes like, it tastes better than attention."*

This is also straight facts. You will not witness people that have self-respect and have experienced great respect and admiration from their peers or supporters do anything solely in an attempt to gain attention.

This is another one of the steps that is going to take some deep internal work. You have to begin to understand that YOU are worthy of respect. Once you believe that you are worthy, you will start respecting yourself more. You will also need to understand how short-lived attention really is.

Remember that post we talked about earlier, the pretend one that you deleted because it only got 5 likes? Well, let's pretend again now that it got 500 likes. All 500 of your FB "friends" saw and liked your picture. How would that change your life? Would it have changed at all? Nope. That attention was as short-lived as the hype over Popeye's chicken sandwich in 2019.

Respect will make you hold yourself to a higher standard regarding your value, energy, passions, and purpose. Choose respect over attention every time.

#92 BOUNDARIES = SELF-TRUST.

ARE YOU SETTING HARD LIMITS?

Setting boundaries will establish your self-trust and reward you with self-confidence.

You've grown so much and developed a lot of awesome new skills. You don't want to risk losing them. Let's build some armor to keep them safe. BOUNDARIES!

Having clearly defined healthy boundaries will establish upfront what behavior you will and won't accept. It also lets other people know what they can expect from you. There are different types of boundaries that you will need to set, and those will be determined by the type of relationship they are concerning. Categorically, the boundaries should be defined physically, emotionally, intellectually, financially- even sexually. These are not in any particular order and they are all equally important to have established.

Once you have your boundaries defined, you'll want to review your relationships. Are there people that are overstepping? Have a conversation with them sooner than later, letting them know your boundary. Make the contract known that you will no longer tolerate them disrespecting the line you've drawn.

Protecting yourself from continuously being violated will give you the extra confidence needed to keep climbing!

#93 EAGLES FLY ALONE.

ARE YOU READY TO SOAR?

To remain at high altitudes, be careful to avoid those that can bring you down.

Like the eagle, true leaders (not just referring to business only here) have the confidence to stand alone. They have courage and compassion. They are able to listen to the needs of their followers and make critical decisions. There is integrity in their intentions and quality behind the actions they take. Why do we all think that eagles are superior?

History proves it. They have the sharpest vision of all the birds. Quick little-known fact – when eagles' age begins to affect their eyesight, they fly higher towards the sun so that the sun can erase the age from their eyes…mind blown. The sharp vision of a leader is what makes them so powerful. They don't lose sight. They continue to soar higher.

I will break the myth though- eagles do not always fly alone. You will see them fly with other eagles, though never with smaller birds.

Most people (small birds) want the easy way for everything. Leaders (you, me, the eagles) we know to *shut the but up!®,* embrace the challenges of reaching those heights, even in the midst of the storms. When the small birds go low, the eagles soar higher.

#94 THANK YOUR HATERS.

WHO MADE YOU A FIGHTER?

If you didn't already, you should go back and read my dedication. It's funny. And true.

I remember a time in middle school. I was getting on the school bus. And this one girl, who for whatever reason felt like it was her calling in life to pick on me, decided that day to tease me about my jeans. Not because there was something wrong with them; they weren't dirty, they weren't ripped. She teased me because she said I wore them all the time. She proceeded to say that I must only own like three pairs of jeans. Maybe I did, maybe I didn't. I don't exactly recall. All I knew was it hurt my feelings. Here I am like 13 being teased over my clothes that I am sure that I worked hard to buy for myself because I never wanted to ask my parents for things that I knew they couldn't afford. Now fast forward to today. I am almost 40, pretty damn successful, and I probably own like 30+ pairs of jeans for no reason, because if I am not in business attire, I am in my standard leggings and tank. Even with that large selection of jeans, some still with tags, would you believe that I still instinctually pick from the same three to five pairs on a regular basis?

Is it out of spite? Subconsciously, possibly. Maybe its just because I love those specific pairs and they make me feel good – could've been the case when I was in middle school also. I often wonder what she is doing with her life. I wonder how many pairs of jeans she has. Maybe I can gift her a few pairs if she needs them.

I am forever grateful for the bullies and haters. *They hate me because they ain't me!* ~~But~~ seriously they do light a fire in you, and it feels really good when you prove them wrong!

Make sure to thank them in your victory speech at the top!

#95 STAY HUMBLE.

DID YOU FORGET WHERE YOU CAME FROM?

Humble, defined as having or showing a low to modest sense of one's own importance.

I have thought about this trendy phrase for quite some time. I seem to always come back to the thought that maybe, just maybe, the person who started this didn't mean it as literal as the definition? Am I the only one that uses words based on their actual definition?

If you take it further and search the definition of a similar word that is often used, *humility* is defined as having a low self-regard and having a sense of unworthiness. I was able to dig deeper and find (finally) that it was added to the definition of *humble* to be free of arrogance. That is what we want! Now we are talking!

When I shared my little story of my middle school bully, I hope that you didn't take my final thoughts as arrogance. It was more along the lines of self-awareness that she was one of my subconscious driving forces that lit a fire inside me to make sure that I was able to provide myself with a wide selection of jeans.

I also share it in hopes of encouraging you to look at your life and find the people and the stories that have shaped you into who you are, to remind you not to forget where you came from. As you achieve success, do not let that turn you into someone you aren't. Be a successful badass ~~but~~ keep free of arrogance!

#96 INVEST IN YOURSELF.

ARE YOU PROVIDING YOURSELF WITH ALL THE TOOLS NECESSARY TO WIN?

Investing in yourself will always provide the greatest return on investment.

By investing in yourself, you are sending a message to the universe that you mean business. It shows that you believe in the value you can provide to the world and that you are confident in the potential you possess.

A lot of the non-monetary ways to invest in yourself we have already covered such as goal setting, living on purpose, building your self-trust and confidence, drinking more water, and consuming more beneficial foods.

There are other ways you need to invest in yourself, though, like this book you are reading (look at you, ahead of the class), seminars and workshops that are specific to your craft, those things on your wanna-do-before-I-die-list, a coach to support your health, fitness, business, and empowerment goals (I can help you with this one), hobbies...the list could go on. These are things that will continue to develop you on your journey.

I also want to touch on investing in things that make you feel good about yourself. Maybe it's a new outfit, haircut, getting a pedicure or massage. When you look good, you feel good and when you feel good, you are unstoppable!

#97 FOLLOW YOUR HEART.

IS IT YOUR HEART THAT IS GUIDING YOU?

Do not let the standards of the world make you change your definition of success.

A reminder- success does not equal money. Success is living our purpose, on purpose, and with passion. We need to be serving our WHY every day fueled by our driving force. If this returns you great monetary gain, that is wonderful. If it comes at the expense of losing yourself, throw it all away and start over.

Running a business is high pressure, especially in a field with so much competition. It is easy to get caught up in the numbers, wanting to be the best, and feeling defeated when you aren't at the top of the charts. I've been there. When things began moving quickly, I didn't recognize it, ~~but~~ I noticed that I was losing myself.

I was so consumed with meeting everyone else's expectations of success that I actually forgot my WHY. I have never slammed on the breaks so hard in my life!

Have you ever heard of someone that is used to winning deciding to fail on purpose? As bizarre as that may sound, I did that. I won good and I failed greater. I went back to my heart, my why, and no matter what people said or thought, I knew I was never going to lose sight of that again.

Follow your heart. I assure you that it is a trustworthy guide.

#98 DREAM BIG.

ARE YOUR DREAMS BIG ENOUGH?

"The biggest adventure you can take in your life is to live the life of your dreams."
―Oprah

Dream so big and set your goals so high that you push yourself to realize the limitless potential you possess. The bigger your dreams, the more obstacles you will have to face, which will, in turn, make your abilities to overcome them stronger and stronger.

These dreams must not only include those tangible goals, ~~but~~ the specific life you want to live, the difference you want to make in the world. They must take into consideration the legacy you want to leave behind.

If you fail to dream big, you will never know what you are capable of. You should also know that because there are so few people who dare to dream big, there is much less competition the higher you rise. If making a difference to you is important, dream big so you can touch more people. Dream big because the will is inside you to make it happen.

~~But~~ *what if I don't achieve my dreams?* Well, I can promise that if you don't believe in yourself, you won't. I can also tell you that if you don't try, you won't either.

Don't forget the small birds; they symbolize small dreams...

#99 TOMORROW IS NOT PROMISED.

WHAT IF TOMORROW DOESN'T COME?

If we're not careful, "later" can become "never."

We have all said the thing above about tomorrow not being promised a time or two in our lives, ~~but~~ do we live by it ourselves?

This last year, while the world watched in horror over the astronomical death toll due to COVID, we all got a reminder of how short life really is.

We know that the only thing truly guaranteed in life is death. So why do we waste what uncertain amount of time we have? I am not sure that we will ever be able to answer that.

For me, the wake-up call is what made me finally start writing this book. A book that, if you were paying attention, I have been joking about writing since at least 2005. A book I didn't start writing until 2021. The realization that we don't have forever also made my desire to help as many people as I possibly can, stronger than ever.

What about you? What about that alarming reminder that tomorrow may not come for you is going to make you take action today? What will you do today since tomorrow might not arrive?

My idea is that you put all that you have learned into motion and go do as much as you can to fulfill your purpose for as long as you can.

#100 HOLD THAT DOOR.

WHO ARE YOU BRINGING WITH YOU?

Now that you have checked your circle and you only have the real ones around you, who are you bringing with you?

If you are an introvert, a loner and it's a one-man show, that's cool too – more power to you.

"No matter how high you climb the ladder of success, never forget those who helped you up."
– Unknown

Most, not all, ~~but~~ most have at least one person- their ride-or-die, that person that would ride until the wheels fell off, then get out and walk with you. Who is that to you? Do not forget about this person. Do not leave them behind.

They may not be an eagle, ~~but~~ their belief in you, the way they have your back, certainly has a lot to do with where you are today.

A wise man once said that no man is an island – we all get our strength and support from interactions with others. Could be strangers, could be your best friend or spouse, could be your administrator. Whoever it is, hold that door and make a seat for them, even if there isn't one there already.

#101 IF IT LOOKS LIKE A DUCK...

ARE YOU IGNORING YOUR GUT?

It's definitely a duck.

Come on! You know, your gut knows. I know…and you still need more proof?

If it looks like a duck,
Swims like a duck,
Quacks like a duck,
IT IS DEFINITELY A DUCK!

There is this part of success that people don't talk about, and it pertains to imposters. Could be other people, could be yourself. Let's chat about both.

First, the Wolf in Sheep's Clothing. They portray a powerful image. They may seem harmless, innocent. They want you to believe they are there to help you. They will use all sorts of different tactics to camouflage their true intentions. Stay aware because they have ulterior motives and will undercut you as soon as you turn your back.

The second one is experiencing imposter syndrome. This is easily described as an overwhelming doubt in your own abilities and intentions. You may feel like you are a fake and a fraud. Those of us who suffer from this will attack ourselves when we are finding it difficult to accept our accomplishments.

Don't fall for either one.

#102 DON'T DRINK THE KOOL-AID.

ARE YOU LETTING THEM INFLUENCE YOU?

If you haven't yet taken some time to think about the question above, do so now. It's important you don't let others convince you to change your course due to their preference or the perceived popularity of an alternate option.

Do you know those people that are always into the latest product or trend? The ones who jump on every bandwagon when they see an opportunity to monetize something? Certainly, we all have at least one FB friend who has sold every MLM product that has been on the market in the last decade. One day they are selling leggings, the next its makeup, and then they move on to adult novelties and Tupperware. Now they've moved on to day trading and cryptocurrency.

Did any of those products speak to their purpose or their passion? If they have solicited their entire audience for each of those different endeavors, who will they have left to support them when they start living on purpose?

In an alternate scenario, think of someone who IS on their path to purpose and it's the road less traveled, so it's not the most popular of destinations. There will be many people trying to pour them a cup along the way of what they will advertise as a more appealing route. Everyone is doing it! They aren't lying. Check the sources, and what you see in your social media feeds are people selling dreams of getting rich off of Dogecoin or day trading when their only professional background is in daycare, or some collections call center.

Don't drink the Kool-Aid, stay in your lane and on your own path, it won't go out of style!

#103 IT'S THE LITTLE THINGS.

ARE YOU FINDING JOY ALONG THE WAY?

If you are staying with your intentions, remaining mindful, and living on purpose, you should be finding joy in all the things along your journey.

Take a moment and think back to the last time you went on a trip somewhere you had never been before. Do you remember thinking about how the air smelled different, the landscape was different, the people's accents were different, the food was different, even the bugs were different? You were so aware because it was all so new. You probably took 200 pictures because you didn't want to miss any of the details. When you came back from your trip, you excitedly rattled off all of the exciting things you saw and did to everyone you know.

You appreciated it because you had never experienced it before.

Walk with your head up while you are on this journey so that you are sure to take note of everything along the way. Document all of it. Live in each moment. Feel how it makes you feel. Appreciate the good days and give yourself grace on bad days. Accept each for what they are. Learn. Grow. Be grateful. Enjoy it.

At the end of the day, it's the little things that matter the most. Find joy in all of them.

#104 THE KISS METHOD ALWAYS APPLIES.

ARE YOU OVERCOMPLICATING THINGS?

Keep it simple, Stupid!

Again, don't shoot the messenger; I didn't call you stupid!

This "method" reminds us not to overcomplicate the process. It is not intended to be complex. As a matter of fact, unless it is absolutely necessary, complexity should be avoided at all costs.

When I was writing out these stairs and building my outline for the book, I was doing research and came across a new age version of the KISS method: *Keep It Super Simple*. You are welcome to use that if you are like me and not a fan of name-calling.

Either way, tuck it in the back of your mind to use as needed. The KISS method always applies!

#105 STAND FOR SOMETHING OR FALL FOR ANYTHING.

ARE YOUR MOVES IN LINE WITH YOUR VALUES?

Be firm in who you are and do not be afraid to stand up for what you believe in.

There aren't many things that I will ever say a person can't do, ~~but~~ one of them is definitely that it is impossible to make everyone happy. If you attempt to, the one person that surely will feel disappointed in the end is yourself.

We learned already the importance of staying true to you. Part of knowing who you are is knowing what you believe in your heart to be right.

Your truth, your character, and your genuine happiness is enough to make a difference in the people's lives that see you for who you really are. They will respect you more for being true to yourself, whether or not you have similar viewpoints.

Everyone is entitled to their own opinions and beliefs. There will be people that disagree with you for what you stand for and try to challenge you; take the challenge. You will either prove your point of view, you both will agree to disagree, or you may learn a new perspective that allows you to grow in your beliefs.

It's important to know what you do believe in and don't define yourself based on someone else's view of the world.

#106 YOU ARE THE AUTHOR OF YOUR OWN STORY.

ARE YOU WRITING A GOOD ONE?

Pick up the pen and write a new chapter.

This is your life and you only have one. Do what you love and do it often. Every day that you are blessed enough to wake up is another chance to change your story.

Don't like the chapter, change it.
Don't like the characters, change them.

Don't like the setting, change it.
Don't like the plot, change it.
Don't like the conflict, change it.
Don't like the theme, change it.

It is your story, and you own the rights to redirect it in any way you choose.

My only recommendation here is that you make sure that you are satisfied with the way it will be projected so that it tells the story of you living your life on purpose.

#107 GREATNESS IS "I AM..."

HOW ARE YOU FINISHING THE STATEMENT ABOVE?

You are great! I hope that you are remembering to tell yourself that every day.

I also hope that you are practicing your daily affirmations.

My favorite part of the day is in the morning when my husband and I both leave the house at the same time – I go straight to the office, and he goes on the first Starbucks run of the day. Yes, we have both already had our morning at-home coffee at this point. I get to the office; I know I have a solid hour before he gets there with the magic bean water and before my admin comes in.

During this time, I journal. I first set my intentions for the day, then write my affirmations. My affirmations are generally pretty consistent unless I am working on a specific manifestation. They look a little something like this:

I am purpose.
I am strong.
I am determined.
I am focused.
I am an inspiration.
I am at peace.
I am courageous.
I am successful.
I am great.

You are great, you need to tell yourself that daily.

#108 THE UNIVERSE WILL ALWAYS SAY "YES."

ARE YOU PUTTING OUT WHAT YOU WANT TO RECEIVE?

Be consistent in your thoughts, believe, be patient, take action, trust, and you will manifest exactly what is meant for you.

The universe is indifferent on whether you are worthy and deserving of your requests. It just says "yes" to your request.

You are about to say I am full of ish because you have been asking for a Ferrari and a million bucks all your life. Let's analyze that against the Law of Attraction then. Just to make you feel better.

Were you consistent in those requests every single day since the first time you put it out there?

Have you believed that you would receive those things every single day since the first time you put them out there?

Have you taken the action that would be necessary to possess those things?

Have you had an unwavering trust that the universe would deliver those things?

I am going to bid a strong "no" to all of the above and go back to the lesson at hand. The universe only says *yes*. If you say that you are broke, the universe says *yes*. If you say that you are in a place of peace, the universe says *yes*.

You decide what the universe is saying *yes* to.

#109 YOU DESERVE IT.

DO YOU BELIEVE THAT?

You deserve to have a life that you are happy about and proud of living.

Have you ever had someone tell you that you are blocking your blessings? How'd you take it?

Recall the person that wanted the million bucks and the Ferrari to fall from the sky ~~but~~ neither showed up. He didn't ever believe it was coming; he never had faith and trust that he deserved it. He never took action to make sure that he acquired those things.

You cannot say you want a better life if you don't have faith and trust that you deserve it. You cannot say you want to love your body if you tell it otherwise, constantly. You can't say that you want to live a life of purpose and passion if you haven't taken the time to identify your WHY and driving force.

You deserve to accomplish all of your hopes and dreams, goals, and aspirations. They are all possible.

Really. You must believe; belief is the key to it all! Until you *shut the but up!®* and believe, with your whole being, nothing else will happen.

#110 YOU GOT THIS.

ARE YOU READY?

It's been a bit of a rollercoaster ride, right?

That's what they all say! Anyone that has made it as far as you, at least.

At this point you have gone through all the things. Done the work. Felt the feelings. Cleared the spaces. Aligned yourself and identified where you are going.

It is still not ever going to be all sunshine and rainbows. You are going to still feel like it's a rollercoaster, ~~but~~ now you are equipped with everything you could need to get back on course if you get knocked off.

Never stop believing in yourself. You got this! You really got this!

YOU GOT THIS!
YOU GOT THIS!
YOU GOT THIS!

#111 IT REALLY IS THAT SIMPLE.
(I didn't say easy.)

HAVE YOU FINALLY…?

I really wish you the best on your journey! You have all the power as long as you believe in yourself and stop making excuses! No "~~but~~" allowed!

xoxo – T. Minor

www.ingramcontent.com/pod-product-compliance
Lightning Source LLC
Chambersburg PA
CBHW070534170426
43200CB00011B/2417